No Challenge
Left Behind

It is often said that children are our future. Not so. We are their future.
The work of education is to create a future for our children.
With that in mind, I dedicate this book to my three children—
Lisa, Suzanne, and Caroline—and to my "grands,"
Will and Lucy. May their future be filled with
hope and possibility.

No Challenge Left Behind

Transforming American Education Through Heart and Soul

Paul D. Houston

Foreword by Terrence E. Deal

A Joint Publication

CORWIN PRESS
A SAGE Company
Thousand Oaks, CA 91320

AMERICAN ASSOCIATION
OF SCHOOL ADMINISTRATORS

Copyright © 2008 by Corwin Press

For information:

Corwin Press	SAGE India Pvt. Ltd.
A SAGE Company	B 1/I 1 Mohan Cooperative
2455 Teller Road	Industrial Area
Thousand Oaks, California 91320	Mathura Road, New Delhi
www.corwinpress.com	India 110 044
SAGE Ltd.	SAGE Asia-Pacific Pte. Ltd.
1 Oliver's Yard	33 Pekin Street #02-01
55 City Road	Far East Square
London EC1Y 1SP	Singapore 048763
United Kingdom	

Printed in the United States of America.

Library of Congress Cataloging-in-Publication Data

Houston, Paul D.
No challenge left behind: transforming American education through heart and
soul/Paul D. Houston.
    p. cm.
"A joint publication with the American Association of School Administrators (AASA)."
Includes index.
ISBN 978–1–4129–6861–4 (cloth)
ISBN 978–1–4129–6862–1 (pbk.)
   1. School management and organization—United States. 2. Educational
leadership—United States. 3. Educational change—United States. I. American
Association of School Administrators. II. Title.

LB2805.H6958 2008
371.2′070973—dc22   2008011867

This book is printed on acid-free paper.

08   09   10   11   12   10 9 8 7 6 5 4 3 2 1

Acquisitions Editor:	Arnis Burvikovs
Editorial Assistant:	Irina Dragut
Production Editor:	Libby Larson
Typesetter:	C&M Digitals (P) Ltd.
Proofreader:	Gail Fay
Indexer:	Rick Hurd
Cover Designer:	Jeffrey Stith
Graphic Designer:	Lisa Riley

CONTENTS

SECTION III. TRANSFORMING PUBLIC EDUCATION:
    CHALLENGES AND SOLUTIONS

SECTION IV. LESSONS FROM THE ROAD

FOREWORD

S aint Paul, "the best man the world possessed, his hair whitened with the labours for the good of men and the glory of God," etched his mark on history through his Epistles. Paul Houston is not a canonized saint, but as a spokesman for the soul and spirit of education he comes close. Several years ago, we published a quote from Paul in our book, *The Wizard and The Warrior:* "At night I relish the opportunity to indulge myself by exploring the unlimited potential of the human spirit. In the morning I don my suit of armor and head off to battle the dark forces at work. I am struggling to integrate the two roles." He speaks for most school administrators in the country who know, deep down, what's right for students but are struggling against a strong riptide pulling schools away from their noble purpose or calling. As an exemplar of heart and courage Paul, each day, exhibits the essence of leadership. In this book he shares his well-seasoned wisdom with the profession he represents.

As a student of leadership, I seldom read the educational administration literature. Most of the writing paints the work of superintendents, principals, and teachers a shade of pale gray when I see it as hot pink. When asked to write this foreword, I received a sample of Paul's "epistles" and then requested the entire volume. I read each one with great joy, effortlessly drawn into a mystical, magical world of teaching, learning, and leading.

A sample of the down-to-earth titles of Paul's stories gives advance notice of what lies ahead: "On Becoming a Hope Pusher," "Barking Up the Right Tree," "The Seven Deadly Sins of No Child Left Behind," "The Road to Hana." The pages are peppered with allegorical language: spirituality, hope, soul, grace, blessing, joy, fun, and fantasy. His writing is inviting and lyrical and his premises compelling. His upbeat message is a welcome antidote to prevailing mechanistic images of schools as factories and students as test scores. Rather than emphasizing rigorous classrooms to see if students measure up, we ought to be championing vigorous places to beckon them in.

My shelves are overflowing with books about leadership and education. This one I'll keep close by. Anytime I begin to doubt the difference schools and leaders can make, I'll pick it up, turn to a story, and remind myself of why I became an educator.

Terrence E. Deal
Professor (ret.)

ACKNOWLEDGMENTS

Even though writing is a singular process, the outcome is never achieved alone. I would like to acknowledge Amy Vogt, Sherri Montgomery, Liz Griffin, and Jay Goldman from the AASA staff, who have had the dubious job of editing my material and keeping me grammatically pure. I am also grateful to the entire staff, governance leaders, and members for supporting my work and allowing my voice to remain my voice. Over the last several years I have developed a relationship with Corwin Press and I am grateful for their support and professionalism in handling my work. Last, and certainly not least, I want to thank the thousands of school leaders who get up every day and go to work to serve the children of America. They are true heroes and heroines in my book and they don't get thanked enough.

Unless noted otherwise, the articles in this book were first published in The School Administrator, *the award-winning monthly magazine of the American Association of School Administrators.*

ABOUT THE AUTHOR

 **Paul D. Houston** served as executive director of the American Association of School Administrators from 1994 to June 2008. He has established himself as one of the leading spokespersons for American public education through his extensive U.S. and international speaking engagements, published articles, and media interviews.

Houston served as superintendent of schools in Princeton, New Jersey; Tucson, Arizona; and Riverside, California. His K–12 education experience also includes working as an assistant superintendent in Birmingham, Alabama, and as a teacher and building administrator in North Carolina and New Jersey. He has also had the pleasure of serving in an adjunct capacity for the University of North Carolina, Harvard University, Brigham Young University, and Princeton University.

Houston completed his bachelor's degree at the Ohio State University and received his master's degree at the University of North Carolina. In 1973, he earned a Doctorate of Education from Harvard University.

In 1991, Houston was honored by the Council of Great City Schools for his leadership in urban education when he received the Richard R. Green Leadership Award. In 1997, he was awarded an honorary Doctorate of Education from Duquesne University. The Hope Foundation honored Houston with the Courageous Leadership Award of 2000. The Horace Mann League presented Houston with the league's 2001 Outstanding Educator Award. In 2008, the American Association of School Administrators granted him the Distinguished Service Award and the American Education Award.

Houston has published more than 200 articles in professional journals. He coauthored the books *The Spiritual Dimension of*

Leadership: 8 Key Principles to Leading More Effectively (Corwin Press, 2006), *The Board-Savvy Superintendent* (Scarecrow Education, 2003), and *Exploding the Myths* (AASA, 1993). His columns have been collected and published in his books *Articles of Faith & Hope for Public Education* (Rowman & Littlefield, 1996), and *Outlook and Perspectives on American Education* (Rowman & Littlefield, 2003).

Houston is coeditor for a series of books on the Soul of Leadership with Corwin Press. Books in the series include *Sustaining Professional Learning Communities* (2008), *Spirituality in Educational Leadership* (2007), *Out-of-the-Box Leadership* (2007), and *Engaging EVERY Learner* (2007).

Houston is committed to advocacy for public education and the children it serves. He is currently writing, speaking, and consulting from his home in Tucson, Arizona.

INTRODUCTION

I have toiled in the vineyards of public education since the late sixties. There is an old joke that says if you remember the sixties you weren't there. Well I was there and I do remember. I also remember the seventies, the eighties, the nineties, and the beginning of the new millennium. Much has changed over that time but much hasn't. And I have learned a lot. One thing I have learned is that Pogo, the cartoon character, was right when he observed that "we are surrounded by insurmountable opportunities." American educators are confronted on all sides by challenges and challengers. But we also have the opportunity to overcome these challenge and to make the world anew through our work

One of my great blessings is that for 14 years as executive director of the American Association of School Administrators I had the opportunity to reflect on all this and to use the bully pulpit of a national position to comment on the good, the bad, and the ugly of the state of education. I have often thought that the schools of America are so much better than the critics think they are, and not as good as those of us who work in them would like to think they are. I have railed against the unwarranted criticism leveled at schools and the expectation that when any problem faces our society, the schools are supposed to handle it. I have also worried that too often our schools aren't reaching the children most in need of a good education and that we slide along offering an education that neither challenges nor uplifts our students.

I have focused much of my observation on the leadership of our schools because that has been my life's work and it is what my "day job" has been. And over the last six years I have watched educators struggle with policy that purports to raise the bar for schools while it lowers the boom on them. I have watched with sadness dedicated professionals struggle to do what is right and what is expected and to try to sort those sometimes competing expectations out. I have

1

said adieu to too many who have left the field of battle prematurely out of frustration and despair.

I have often said I believe in the American dream because I have lived it. And I got to live it because of the public schools of this country. American public education has been the cornerstone of our democracy and without it, there is no American public. So I have fought against those who would destroy it by design or disregard. One of the things that has changed since I began my career back in the sixties is that many of the idealists of that period have become the cynics of today so that public education today must not only worry about its enemies—it must worry about its friends who have given up on the possibilities and who fail to understand what is at stake.

The idealism of the sixties was about equality and opportunity. That is still the challenge but it is so much more subtle now. Then, it was overcoming Jim Crow laws and overt racism. Today, the racism is dressed in prettier clothes and the laws that purport to help the poor and minority unconsciously maim them by narrowing possibilities through the results of a cheap assessment system built on bubbled-in answers and bubble-headed ideas of how to make education better.

Meanwhile, the "flattened earth" and the challenge of global competition, the widening gulf between those who have and those who don't, the explosion of information that comes at learners with the speed of light, and the need to sort the wheat of wisdom from the chaff of misinformation has made the educational process so much more complex than it once was in those good old smoke-filled days of the sixties.

And school leaders have had to confront these challenges without adequate support or resources. They have been asked to make bricks without straw as they work in an environment that requires results without resources and solutions without support.

So I have tried to offer guidance and reinforcement through the insights I have gathered from all around me. Those who know me well know I am nothing if not eclectic in my thinking and my sources of insight. In the last few years I have written and spoken more and more from a spiritual perspective because I truly believe the work of education is "soul work" because it touches the deepest parts of who we are. We must be attuned to the fact the work we do comes from the soul and through the heart. Our work is not mechanical—it is organic and it is truly a mission. We are called to do what we do and we must be in touch with that calling to be effective. So sometimes I tend to focus on the affect as much as the effect of our work.

This book is a collection of these observations from the last few years. In many ways it represents a culmination of the work I decided to do back in those kaleidoscopic and tie-dyed sixties. My hair isn't as long as it was then, and it certainly isn't as dark, but I would like to think that as my hair has lightened, my understanding of our work, its challenges, and its opportunities has become more enlightened.

This book is divided into four sections. The first focuses on what I call the "building blocks of leadership." These are certainly not totally inclusive but offer a wide range of views on what it means to be a leader and how one might approach this work. Some of my views are probably held by a minority of one and might be seen as eccentric. I hope you will also find them provocative.

The second section focuses on the job I know best in education—that of superintendent. For over 30 years I have either been a superintendent or have headed the national organization that supports their work. So you must forgive me if I have built up a few opinions over that time. One is that we must stop viewing the job as being a "superintendent of schools" and begin seeing it as a superintendent of learning and education. It is not about the place; it is about the processes and relationships that take place in that place we call school.

The third section offers some of my views of how we might face the challenges of transforming education with a different approach. I have a pretty simple idea for transforming schools—we must make them places kids want to be. That must come from creating a learning situation that is engaging and meaningful—and maybe just a bit joyful. I think for America to survive in the global environment it has to get back to what it has always done best—promoting creative thinkers who challenge the status quo and conventional thinking. That would be a good start at transforming our schools.

The last section I am calling "Lessons From the Road." My work has been the work of a warrior—but often it has been as a "road warrior." I have lost and worn out more suitcases than most people have seen, stayed in more hotels than a traveling salesman, and logged more flight miles than most pilots. But what I have tried to do is extract meaning from these sometimes seemingly meaningless experiences. Since I express myself most vividly through metaphor and story, this road warrior part of my life has served as a rich resource and fodder for my views on education and leadership.

I can honestly say that the writing I did to create this book has been a labor of love. It comes to you from the warmth of my heart and the depths of my soul. I love the work I have been privileged to do and those I have been blessed to stand side to side with over these last four decades. Yes, we *are* surrounded by insurmountable opportunities, but when I get discouraged I go back to the words of William Faulkner as he accepted the Nobel Prize for literature. He said that he believed that mankind would not only survive but prevail. I believe in no less for the educators who care so much about their work and their children.

SECTION I

THE BUILDING
BLOCKS
OF LEADERSHIP

1

SO? . . . BUT NOT
SO WHAT!

I was talking with a friend recently when he confided he was having a problem developing one of his talents because he was afraid he might be criticized by others for not doing it well. I introduced him to a powerful philosophy I have worked out over the years that I commend to you as well. Unlike most philosophies, it is simple, easy to understand, and easy to remember. It's one word: "So?"

Don't get me wrong. It is not "So what?" which is a very different philosophy. So what is a dismissive view of the world. It is aggressive and leaves no room for learning. So what just says you aren't listening and that you probably think you know better than the other person and you have no real interest in what they have to say. It is the verbal equivalent of putting your hands over your ears and repeating "lalalalalala."

So is a much deeper view of the world. So is based on two principles—discernment and detachment. Discernment is necessary because it is important to listen to what others say and think. That means you have to take in lots of information and then you have to consider it. That is particularly true in the work we do.

DISCERNING MINDS

Leadership is all about connection and the fastest way to break connection is to fail to listen to others. So listening and caring about what you are hearing is crucial. But it is a good idea to use some discernment once that is done. I can't imagine everything you hear during the day is useful or even that it all makes good sense. A lot of what I heard in the superintendent's office was spectacularly idiotic and a lot more didn't really help me with my work. I have to admit some of that came from my own mouth. The point here is that all of us aren't wise all the time. You have to filter what is said and suggested.

I also can't imagine every criticism you hear is worth adopting or taking seriously. You have to discern whether what you are hearing is worthy of your effort to adapt and adopt. It has been my experience that some of what I get from others in the way of suggestions and ideas is valuable and needs to be taken seriously. Other thoughts are best left dormant. Discerning minds want to know, but they don't always feel the need to act.

Attachment comes when you take in what others think as the way you feel you should live your life. You choose to accept their judgments and views as better than your own and then you feel you need to follow their drumbeat. Detachment comes when you learn that others' ideas and judgments are just that—ideas and judgments. They are no better or worse than your own. Certainly, not much good can come from you taking them in and living your life based upon them. In fact, a lot of the unhappiness I have observed in life has come from an individual's inability to detach from what others think.

Detachment doesn't mean you don't feel. You don't have to be numb or dumb. You just have to refuse to own the junk mail that others send you. Do you save all the spam in your inbox? Detachment is simply a way of deleting the spam.

SUCCINCT PHILOSOPHY

So that brings us back to "so." When I laid out my philosophy, my friend laughed and suggested I might be on to something. He marveled at the economy of what I was offering and suggested it might be the shortest philosophic statement he had heard. In fact, it is one of the shortest words in the English language—bested only by "I" as the shortest. And that is the opposing philosophy to so.

The I philosophy leaves no room for listening because no one else is important. I (see, it is hard to talk without using the word) have observed too often I appears in the middle of superIntendent.

It is pretty easy, when you are the big cheese, to think it is all about you. It also appears much too often in the middle of those the superintendent deals with.

If so is about discernment and detachment, then I is about selfishness and self-centeredness. It assumes Galileo was wrong and that I, not the sun, exist in the center of the universe. Sadly, many start out with a "you" philosophy, but when one is totally selfless, it often leads to feeling abused and used. The you morphs into I and selflessness becomes selfishness. While it starts with self-protection, it quickly becomes destructive to others.

MIDDLE GROUND

So there is a middle way—the so way. It can take many forms: "So, what can I do for you?" (being selfless with thought attached); "So, what's so important about that?" (looking before buying); "So, let's look at it another way" (opening the discussion to alternative ideas).

So is a conjunction or an adverb. It connects things—sews them together if you will—and it describes. It holds a place in the center of things, but it can also emphasize the quality of an experience. It can make things bigger ("it was so awesome!"). And better ("it was so wonderful!").

So, where was I? I realize if we could master the concept of so, I really think folks would be freed up to do what they are capable of doing. They would not be hemmed in by the limiting beliefs of others. They would not get so distressed about the challenges life offers and they could become unstuck in ways that allow them to be powerful. You might recall the empowering orders offered by Captain Picard on *Star Trek:* "Make it so."

Education has to be about lifting limitations on ourselves and on others. So what's stopping us?

2

FINDING OUR VOICE

My daughter Suzanne has wanted to be an actress since high school. She was in every school play, majored in drama in college, taught drama after college, did summer theatre and dinner theatre, and finally put herself on the line and went to New York City to pursue her dream.

But before she acted, she sang. In fact, as a small child she had this BIG Broadway voice and she would sing along to the car radio and you would have thought some large lady was singing in the backseat instead of a diminutive five-year-old. She boomed it so that when she sang, "The sun will come out tomorrow," you believed it!

She was lucky to go to school in Princeton, New Jersey, which has an amazing vocal music program that starts in kindergarten and just gets better and better as the kids get older. But a funny thing happened with Suzanne. As she got older, her voice got better but it got smaller. As she was trained to sing "properly" and learned to blend her voice with others as part of an ensemble, she let go of her BIG voice. As her harmony improved, her individual talent was smothered. She still had a beautiful singing voice, but it just wasn't so special anymore and "tomorrow" sounded a long way off.

Recently, I was in New York and Suzanne suggested we go to see *Mamma Mia* because her current vocal coach was one of the stars. We did and were able to go backstage after the show for a guided tour by the coach and star. As we were walking on the stage, Suzanne's coach talked about her work with Suzanne and how proud she was that Suzanne had had to learn to "belt" (which is "Broadway speak" for having that BIG voice).

The coach asked me if I had heard her use that newly acquired voice and at first I said no, but then I realized I had—when she was five. I mentioned she sang that way when she was young but hadn't for a long time. The coach said that Suzanne had had to find her "natural voice," which was the BIG one, and that school had taught her how to sing properly but not naturally. The coach then told us about her own journey as a singer and that she had finally found a way back to her own voice.

A Voice Inside

What a powerful lesson for us all. Shouldn't education be about helping children find their own natural gifts? Shouldn't we help them find their own "voice"? Shouldn't we do that for ourselves? How many of us use our "natural voice" as leaders? How many of us have the confidence and courage to lead in our own voice? Are we willing to write and speak in our own voice? Do we act from our own voice—that one that we know leads us to truth in action?

We all have that small, still voice inside us that acts as a guide. Do we listen to that voice? Would we have as much chaos with out-of-control politics or out-of-the-mind reform if we had more leaders using their own voices? Shouldn't we be speaking more about reforms that don't make sense, which come from "reformers" who know nothing about teaching and learning? Shouldn't we be saying more about the need to solve the right problems rather than the obvious ones? Shouldn't we be singing loudly that if we lose public education we lose any chance for a sunny tomorrow for America?

Leaders are expected to lead, but they are expected to lead authentically. Leadership comes from the inside out. It derives its strength from the essence of who and what we are as humans. To lead effectively, we have to know what our own voice sounds like and then we have to use it.

In Harmony

But leadership is also about helping others find their own voices. What do we do to help our staff and teachers discover and use their voices?

One of the leader's greatest frustrations is our need to try to get everyone singing from the same page. Singing the same song is good, but if they are all singing the same notes it is pretty boring. You need a variety of tones to make the music interesting.

Suzanne had wonderful preparation for blending her voice with others. She is amazing at harmonizing. But her gift is also the ability to belt a solo. Don't we want all our teachers using their gifts to greatest effect? Wouldn't education be more effective if we could encourage them to use what they have and what they know?

We are living and working in a time when schools and learning are being minimalized and marginalized. Education is being equated with the results of norm-referenced tests—seeing who can repeat a few limited notes most accurately. It is also focusing on what you know, not what you can do. I read music, but you would never want me to sing for you. Yet if we really expect our children to learn, they have to be let out of the box and allowed to find their own expression and be encouraged to make the music.

Real learning will happen when leaders use their voices to help teachers find theirs so that students can sing with openness and freedom. The balancing act for us is to make sure they learn the notes and know how to blend their voice with others without giving up their unique gifts.

The meaning of "educate" comes from the Latin "educare" which means "to bring forth." The essence of what we must do as leaders is to use our abilities to help our teachers bring forth all that is within them so that they can do the same for children. If we can do that, the sun really will come out tomorrow.

This essay received an Award of Merit in the writing category in the National School Public Relations Association's 2007 Publications and Electronic Media Contest.

3

BREAKING AWAY

W hen my youngest daughter, Caroline, was a baby, she would sometimes accidentally link her fingers together so that one hand was holding the other. She would begin to pull and shake her hands, trying to free herself. The more she struggled, the more frustrated she became.

Finally, being the good father, I would help her untangle herself. Of course, she really didn't require my help. All she had to do was open her fingers and let go.

Thinking about that now, years later, I can see how adults aren't very different from the children we observe. We constantly tangle ourselves up in knots of our own creation, and we pull and push trying to free ourselves when all we have to do is release ourselves from our own entanglements. Poet William Blake described this condition as "mind-forged manacles," being held captive by the handcuffs we create for ourselves.

Ellen Langer, in her wonderful little book *Mindfulness,* describes the process of this creation as a part of our learning experience. We learn as children what is right, what is wrong, what is proper and what is not. We learn to sort and categorize. While this is an important part of our maturation, it also begins to shut us down to other possible ways of seeing the world.

The ultimate shutdown is found in the education system itself. As it focuses on specified outcomes, it narrows the choices the learner has of looking at the world. Langer describes this process as the creation of "mindlessness."

DESTRUCTIVE SYMBOLS

As I look at our culture today, I detect the ravages of mindlessness on every front. Some comes from allowing symbols and slogans to cut us off from being open to broader possibilities.

Take the flag and the cross as examples. In the interest of full disclosure, I must tell you I wear a cross and proudly own a number of flags. The problem comes when we mistake the displaying of these symbols as a way of claiming all they stand for. It is not enough to show the flag and then use your own professed patriotism as a means of shutting off others' views of what it means to be patriotic.

Some would see it as patriotic to support our troops by not raising questions about the war they are fighting. Others would see our troops best supported by bringing them home. Without weighing in on which is right, both of these positions and others between them should be discussed and considered. That would allow for mindfulness.

Likewise, the wearing of a cross suggests an allegiance to one religion held dear by millions around the world. Yet simply displaying that object without giving ongoing thought of what the man who first had to wear a cross stood for is a mindless action. It is hard to wear a cross with sincerity without worrying about how loving, compassionate, and forgiving you have to be on a daily basis. The bar is set pretty high and those who would cast stones are in danger of casting judgment on themselves.

In education, we carry on in ways that endanger us to behave mindlessly. I recently heard a highly intelligent educator suggest we should take unemployed engineers and retool them to teach math and science so our children could grow up to become engineers.

Think about this for a second. Does it make sense? If there aren't jobs for engineers today, will there be jobs tomorrow? Or are we suggesting that we need to ramp up the training of children for high-tech jobs when the competition in Asia is working for one-fifth of the going salaries here? What are we training them for and won't economics come into play? What will be the ultimate outcome here? And it goes on and on.

We teach children foreign languages in high school, long after their neural wiring for acquiring languages has peaked. We want our children to be globally competitive, but we cut back on bilingual programs and make the children who already have another language stop using it so they can learn English. Because a lot of the globe doesn't speak English and our children need other perspectives, aren't we hurting ourselves if we are to remain competitive?

INFLATED EGOS

Within our own profession we wear the symbols of our office as if that makes us leaders. I have heard some of our peers refer to themselves in third person as if that makes them more important. Our titles and our egos aren't important—how we work with others and how mindful we remain are.

Langer suggests mindfulness is the key aspect of leadership. She describes it as the ability to connect to the environment and to others. Above all, it is to remain open and aware. Her research indicated that people who demonstrate these qualities are magnets for others. They are good leaders.

Jim Collins, in *Good to Great,* described Level 5 leaders (the ones who were most effective in creating greatness) as being transparent so those in the organization get the credit for the greatness. In the Eastern teaching of Taoism, there is a thought that leaders should behave in ways so that when the work is done the people will say, "We did it ourselves." This calls for a different kind of ego and a different kind of vision and a different frame of mind.

Educational leaders must get past the simple symbols and the "either/or" mentality that permeates our culture and lead others to discover the greatness that already lies within them. The fact is our children are most limited by the narrow definitions we put on learning—the "mental handcuffs," to paraphrase Blake. I'm pretty sure that if we open our minds, our brains won't fall out—all that will happen is that we will break away from the chains that hold us back.

4

RISKING OUR
SIGNIFICANCE

In my friend Dawna Markova's wonderful poem "I Will Not Die an Unlived Life," she writes about the need to "risk (our) significance." That line always has struck me as I have thought about how hard it is for any of us to risk our significance, but that is especially true for leaders.

Whether we want to admit it or not, most of us ended up in leadership positions because of the pursuit of our significance. Sure, we went into administration because we wanted to make a difference in the lives of children and to make the world a better place and for all the other high-minded reasons that are both true and convenient.

But the reality is that we could have done all that by taking a lot of other paths. We could have fulfilled these high purposes by becoming missionaries, going to work in a homeless shelter, or staying in the classroom.

Instead we chose to take on successively more challenging and more significant roles in administration. We did it to have a greater impact and we did it because of our own needs. Could we just admit that we are administrators, in part, because it feeds that portion of ourselves that needs to feel important? And that ambition is both a blessing and a curse. It has driven us to new heights, but in gaining the high ground we risk losing a sense of why we were climbing. We tend to hold tighter to the ground we have gained for fear of falling.

APPEARING FOOLISH

Having reached the goal of being significant (and it is my opinion there is no position in America today more significant than a public school leader), why then would we want to risk that very significance? That is the interesting paradox of leadership. Just as you can only truly lead by being willing to serve, you can only truly reach a level of significance by being willing to give it up.

What are some of the ways we can risk our significance? One is by being willing to appear foolish. The power of leadership is not in the breadth of our answers but in the depth of our questions. I had a board member say he wanted to compliment me. He said, "What I like about you is that you are willing to ask the dumb question." And you know what? That was a compliment for it is only in asking dumb questions that you can get to the smart answers.

How many times have we been in situations where we were confused and yet no one was willing to stop and ask some of the basic questions that would lead to clarity? Smart people have led nations to war because no one was willing to stop and ask the dumb questions. School reform efforts have failed because no one was willing to stop and ask why something was being tried as a solution, when the problem was something entirely different.

No Child Left Behind—now recognized, even by those who created it, as having flaws needing revision—was passed because members of Congress didn't ask some "dumb" questions like "Is it possible to test people into being smarter?" or "Is it really accountability if we are comparing different groups of children?" or "Can we really make certain we are not leaving poor children behind when we won't deal with the poverty that caused them to be behind in the first place?" These dumb questions could have led to smarter answers.

Another way of risking our significance is by failing to act. I would submit that more children have been harmed by our failure to do something than by our doing the wrong thing to them. Acting without thought isn't the right way. But thinking without acting won't get us very far either.

We need to demonstrate a sense of urgency around the issue of educational improvement. This is the only childhood our children have. We need to make certain that it counts for something. Things loom larger in childhood. Dangers are greater, obstacles higher, and time is more significant. At my age, time has sped up. For me a year is but 1/60th of my life. For a fourth grader it is 10 percent of his or her experience.

For children, time goes slower. A year with a bad teacher or hounding by a bully is a big part of their total existence. As their defenders and shapers, we must risk our significance by acting with a greater sense of urgency.

RIGHTEOUS INDIGNATION

By far the greatest threat to our significance is the need to act courageously. One great paradox of leadership is that our daily effectiveness grows from our ability to compromise and find common ground. But ultimately, the path to the future is paved with our willingness to be unreasonable in our passion and unwavering in our commitment to what is right. And when you act with passion and commitment, you will sometimes break some china—but that is ultimately why you became a leader. Significance comes from your willingness to make a difference.

Leadership, to be effective, must be wrapped in righteous indignation. We must become indignant about the conditions that surround our children. We must become indignant about the wrong-headed reforms that wrap unique individuals into one-size-fits-all garments. We must become indignant about politicians and interest groups who would destroy public education in the name of saving it.

Dawna Markova's poem speaks to our not living in "fear of falling or catching fire," and she goes on to suggest we let our hearts become "a wing, a torch, a promise." She ends the poem by stating that "I chose to risk my significance, to live so that which came to me as seed, goes on as blossom and that which came to me as blossom goes on as fruit."

Leadership is taking seed to blossom and blossom to fruit, and the first step is to be willing to lose what we have worked so hard to gain. Only by letting go do we learn to fly.

5

DAILY BLESSINGS

A few months ago I saw a homeless person by the side of the road holding a sign with an unexpected message. Instead of the usual phrases, "Will work for food" or "Stranded, please help," his sign read simply, "Blessings anyway." His message caught me short because given his personal situation I did not expect him to be offering blessings.

This encounter started me thinking that often our lives are blessed in strange and unexpected ways. Sometimes the darkest moments in our lives hold unexpected blessings because they offer us the opportunity to peer from the shadows that surround us and reveal to us the brightness we are granted so much of the rest of the time. That homeless person's sign was a reminder to those who saw it that, no matter how desperate his own situation, he could be a source of blessing to others. Could we do less ourselves?

Shortly after that incident, Jean Reid, the wife of C. J. Reid, who is one of our senior managers at AASA, passed away suddenly and unexpectedly. Her death hit all who knew her and C. J. with the force of losing one of our own close relatives. Part of the loss was due to her unique personality. All of us who met Jean felt as if we had known her our whole lives. Her personality and life force were so strong, she blew into our lives like a benevolent hurricane and our landscape was permanently altered by her presence. Her laugh was contagious and she saw humor and humanity in everything around her.

STORY SHARING

As we sat at her memorial service on a magnificent spring afternoon in Alexandria, Virginia, I kept thinking of a line from a James
Taylor song, "So the sun shines on this funeral, just the same as on
a birth, the way it shines on everything that happens here on earth."
This was reinforced by the fact we were sitting as an AASA family
and two of our staffers were moving toward the upcoming births of
their first children. There we were, bookended by the complete circle of life—birth and death. While each is a dramatic milestone,
they mark but two days in the thousands we are given. Each is out
of our control—birth determined by our parents and death by cos-
mic circumstances.

It is all the days between that we have responsibility over. The
question becomes how we choose to live them. During the memorial service, those offering Jean's eulogy observed that, at her core,
she was a storyteller and that you couldn't be around her without
her telling stories, even if it only involved a recent trip to the supermarket. They went on to observe that storytellers don't live lives
that are more interesting lives—they live lives that are "wide
awake." Storytellers have to be present in the moment for it is only
then that they can observe life as an unfolding story that bears
repeating. And in the repeating they are living lives of celebration
because they are able to celebrate all that seems so ordinary but yet
is quite extraordinary.

I often have advocated that leaders must learn to be storytellers.
For in telling stories one can connect to the core humanity of others
and make life accessible. It presents your humanity to the humanity
of those you need to influence and connects you to their essence in
the only way that counts—soul to soul.

But as I heard Jean eulogized, it seemed I had been missing the
point all these years. It is not the stories that make the connection, it
is the being present that makes one a leader of others. The great
irony of the work of leadership is that so much of it seems to be centered in the past—building on what has been or correcting past problems or in the preparation for the future and for building that which
is not already created. Yet the real work of leadership occurs in the
space between yesterday and tomorrow—the present.

CONNECTING HUMANITY

I am reminded of the observation I once heard that "yesterday is gone, tomorrow has not arrived; all we have is today and that's why we call it the present." The reality is that each day we have is a present that allows us to connect to our humanity and to the humanity of those around us. Leadership is not about bottom lines, test scores, buildings built, people hired or fired, or the thousand other things that take up our time.

Leadership is about our ability to make a connection to another person. And we do that by staying in touch with our own humanity and with our own awareness of our fragile place on this earth. It is good that we not get too caught up in our own significance because whatever significance we have comes from the connections we create rather than from the positions we hold.

Being in the moment, staying centered—being present is the best present we could give ourselves in this or any holiday season. Being present allows us to pay attention, to see the little signs by the side of the road that remind us that regardless of where we are or who we are or what we are facing, our duty as humans and as leaders is to offer blessings to others.

The meaning of blessings can range from giving permission to pieces of good fortune and miracles. My friend Bill Milliken, when leaving the company of others, always says, "Blessings." Now I know why. He is giving the most important gift one can offer another. In fact, it is the role of leaders to bestow their blessings on others by granting permission for people to become what they can and by doing so to allow miracles to happen. Even on those days we may wish we had stayed in bed, it is good to know our presence can offer blessings anyway.

6

LIVING IN A JERRY SPRINGER WORLD

Ok, I admit it. I have watched Jerry Springer on occasion. It is a guilty pleasure. I don't know if his popularity is because we know people like the ones he has on his show, because we don't know people like the ones he has, or because we are just glad we aren't on the show ourselves.

The Springer show has come to represent the extremes in our society—perversion, unlikely pairings, lying, cheating, and what have you. Come to think of it, kind of reminds me of Washington, D.C. And that's the point.

As I look at what has evolved in our society over the past few years I sometimes think we are all living in a Jerry Springer world. On one hand we have seen a coarsening in our society of what is acceptable. Our public discourse has become laced with words of four letters. We see the vice president, a hero of social conservatives, dropping the "F bomb" on a senator in the Senate chamber itself. And not much is made of it. Just the way things are.

Liberal Hollywood has been roundly criticized, and justifiably so, over the direction it has taken with much of our entertainment to the point that AASA even considered a position calling for a tax on the "toxic culture." The theory behind the measure was that our children are victimized by movies, records, and video games that teach and glorify violence and that you pay a price in terms of what parents and schools must contend with as a result of this toxic influence. So those who perpetrate it should have to pay to offset the influence.

The idea was too complicated to gain much traction, but the fact that it was even considered says much about where we are right now. Further, much of the toxicity of our culture as it affects children comes from our cultural fascination with violence, but as a culture we often seem more upset with sex than we are with violence—so what do we tackle?

So much was made of Janet Jackson's costume malfunction that it changed the way the Federal Communications Commission looks at television programming. This has led to programs being pulled off the television or modified for fear of incurring a steep fine. It is hard to keep up with what has happened lately and it is hard to know which side to come down on. My social liberal tendencies are at war with my conservative grandfatherly instincts. My libertarian views of feeling government should stay out of people's lives clashes with my Christian values. I think many of us are torn.

BACKWARDS LOOKING

Not long ago I was watching a reprise of the first Super Bowl in 1966 and was surprised to see the men in the crowd wearing white shirts and ties, while many women wore suits and hats. White shirts, ties, and pillbox hats at a football game? Yes, that is the way it was. And there is something in most of us that longs for that simpler, more genteel time. On the other hand, most of the minorities present that day were on the field of play—few were sitting in the stands—reminding us once again that the "good old days" weren't so good for everyone and that progress is never achieved by stepping backwards.

But some things are pretty clear at this point. We won't be wearing ties to a football game anytime soon. Profanity and sexuality will be a part of our culture for the foreseeable future. And as a nation we will continue to debate which is more obscene—Janet Jackson's breast, or a "shock and awe" military attack with collateral damage.

What worries me in the midst of all this is that on Jerry Springer you have the guests, who seem to have come from some parallel universe where bad teeth are a mark of beauty, but you also have the audience. And the audience isn't much different from us. The most obscene thing about Jerry Springer isn't the poor lost souls who share their horrible secrets with the world—it's the audience that sits there and hoots and howls and begs for more or, on the other extreme, shouts down the guests, preventing them from explaining themselves. We have become a culture of hooters and howlers who egg on bad behavior.

I have become increasingly concerned not just about our toxic culture but also our culture of censorship. First, I think that creating laws or rules will not change behavior. It is like Austin Powers yelling, "Oh, behave." You can yell it, but it won't happen. We don't need constitutional amendments to direct behavior. We need changes in personal constitutions. Further, who are the censors and what do they know? Do I want James Dobson or Jerry Falwell or Larry Flynt determining what I see and hear? Do I want Orrin Hatch or Ted Kennedy to determine what is appropriate for me?

DEEPER CONVERSATIONS

I think I reached my own tipping point recently when I read about the attack on SpongeBob SquarePants and the accusations he was promoting "alternative" lifestyles because they had used him in a tolerance promotion. Hey, it's a cartoon! Lighten up! Were Mickey and Minnie promoting cohabitation? (As far as I know, they never married.) The real obscenity is attacking tolerance.

I think we do need to have a deeper conversation with each other about the kind of culture we want and we need to include everyone in the discussion—even SpongeBob SquarePants and his "deviant" friends. And we need to work on our parenting skills. Maybe if we raised our children with some support and structure, they wouldn't be so affected by the culture that surrounds them. And maybe we need to understand that in a Jerry Springer world, the problems cease when the audience stops watching. If we don't like how our world is, we need to become part of the solution and stop being part of the problem.

7

THE SAMURAI
SUPERINTENDENT

For more than a thousand years the Samurai warrior in Japan carried a tradition. While our Western notion of the Samurai conjures up a fierce fighter wielding a massive sword in battle, the real tradition of the Samurai is much more nuanced and appropriate for today's leaders.

The core of the Samurai is one of ethics and service. In fact, the meaning of Samurai is "men of service." And service should be at the core of our work, too.

The code of the Samurai involved total devotion to a set of moral principles. The goal was to perform their duty and exhibit spiritual power. While the Samurai were warriors, they were also poets, artists, and philosophers.

The principles comprising the code of the Samurai would be useful for today's leaders. The first principle was to show duty and loyalty. How many leaders today have lost their sense of duty to their children, their communities, and, yes, even to their boards? How do we express our loyalty and fealty of service? It might involve going beyond adherence to the rules to a much deeper level of commitment to those around us and to the sacred work we have chosen.

PAIRED PRINCIPLES

The second set of principles involves justice and morality, an unusual pairing. Can you be moral without exhibiting justice? Isn't justice based on a set of moral principles? The Samurai also needed to demonstrate complete sincerity in all things. Sincerity is authenticity— being real in word and deed.

The Samurai always were supposed to show compassion. Compassion is composed of equal parts empathy and respect. You must feel another's pain and honor that person's values with your respect.

Samurai also were to demonstrate heroic courage and honor. Have we or our colleagues cut corners to get something done? Courage must be coupled with compassion to yield a sense of honor. You can be courageous without honor, which just makes you a bad winner. You may prevail but without an inner gyroscope guiding you to the proper end. You can be honorable without courage, which leaves you a gracious loser. Our task today is to make our systems and our children winners. To do so without adequate support takes courage. Yet we also must win graciously.

The Samurai accepted responsibility for their words and actions. That is the task of leadership. Many of us like the glory of being in charge and the power we think comes with the title. Do we also revel in the responsibility it entails? That is far more than being responsible for the test scores or making the budget balance. We have the children of our community and their future in our hands. We are responsible for the welfare of our employees.

The essence of ethical behavior is to take responsibility for our actions. The Samurai knew that with power came responsibility. So should we.

Part of the code of the Samurai was to be prepared to die. They believed it was only in being prepared to die that you could truly live. A critical decision for any leader is to know which hills you are prepared to die on and to know you can't die on all of them. Making your choices about what is core to your own code is the first step toward being liberated to do what you must. Then you can live.

The Samurai believed the sword was in the man. The essence of who we are—not the weapons we might hold—makes us brave and makes us effective. A key weapon for the Samurai was the "stillness of mind" that would allow them to be centered and present. In the midst of battle they could still their minds and go to the inner source to find their truth and find their way. They believed that to know life in every breath is the way of the warrior.

How can we, as leaders, find that stillness of mind that allows us to see what is not there and to anticipate what is to come? I think it is found, as the Samurai knew, in knowing life in every breath.

PERFECT BLOSSOMS

A Zen proverb says there are no truths, there are only stories. In that vein, some of my understanding of the Samurai comes from *The Last Samurai*. In the movie the Samurai leader Katsumoto says, "The perfect cherry blossom is a rare thing. You could spend your whole life looking for it and it would not be a wasted life." While he sought perfection in his way of life, he also sought to find the perfect cherry blossom so he could complete a poem he had worked on his whole life.

Katsumoto teaches the Tom Cruise character, Nelson Algren, how to become a Samurai. He warns the way of the Samurai is not easy. Algren wonders if a man can change his destiny. Katsumoto replies, "I believe a man does what he can until his destiny is revealed." The exchange perfectly captures the challenge we have as superintendents or as any kind of leader. Our work is not easy, but it is the work we must do as our destiny is revealed to us.

Near the end of the movie Katsumoto dies, and in his final moments he sees a grove of cherry trees with thousands of blossoms—all perfect—and he finds the final truth. Our duty as school leaders is to search for the perfection that is already inside of each of our children. A worthy life.

8

THE AXIS OF EVIL

E vil has a strange effect on us—the more we think about it, the more it pulls us in and covers us with the ashes of its darkness. The more we see it in others, the more likely it is to manifest in us. Since 9/11, the discussion of evil has become a national pastime. Sadly, the more evil we see in others, the greater chance it will appear in us.

In his State of the Union address, President Bush referred to an "axis of evil." He also has frequently talked about the "evildoers" who oppose us. While we have already defeated one of the axis members, we are finding how adhesive evil can be: When you hit, it pulls you in. This has led me to think about the axis of evil that I see in our own country and what dangers it represents to leaders.

The first leg of the evil axis is fear. In an effort to rally our country to overcoming another axis of evil, a former president said, "The only thing we have to fear is fear itself." The danger of fear is that it enslaves you. By simply talking about fear, we feed it. Now we are told that we are in a permanent war against terrorism and that it is not a question of whether but merely when and where the evildoers will strike.

Yet even in 2001 we lost many more citizens to cars and guns than we did to terrorism. Many more kill themselves than are killed by terrorists. We even have an elaborate color code to tell us if our fears should be merely elevated or heightened. We have more intimate encounters with airline security personnel than we have with our significant others. We started a war over supposed weapons of mass destruction when we have more of these weapons ourselves than the rest of the world put together. The question is, Whom should we fear?

A THIN DISTINCTION

Good leadership never should rest itself on fear. In education we have seen the fear of violence lead us to make our schools less welcoming places and therefore less safe places for students. We have seen our fear of failure cause us to jump on the accountability bandwagon. We know that multiple-choice tests are the lowest possible denominator of learning and that an over-reliance on that to the exclusion of other measures narrows learning. We shouldn't fear accountability, but we also shouldn't use it to create fear in others.

Cognitive scientists tell us that fear limits our cognitive abilities. We must guard against our country and our profession standing on fear as our motivator. Leadership is about opening the possibilities to people and learning is about setting people free from the darkness of their fears and ignorance.

The second leg of the axis of evil is arrogance. This is tough because there is a thin line between confidence and arrogance. My simple distinction is that a confident person thinks he is as good as anyone else; an arrogant person thinks he is better. When you act without regard for what others think or without care about the consequences of your actions on others, then you are arrogant. When you act unilaterally without including others in what affects them, you are being arrogant. And arrogance begets an interesting reaction—resistance, dislike, and rebellion.

School leaders must particularly guard against arrogance. When you are the leader of an organization, you have a great deal of real or perceived power. You must be very guarded on how you use it. If you carry forth your power without including others in the process or without caring what your actions might do to others, you are behaving arrogantly.

How do I know this? Because I have done it. We all have from time to time. We have all used shortcuts to get things done or taken actions that made us look good but may not have enriched the lives around us. Acting without regard to others is the first step on the road to becoming evil ourselves.

A CONSUMING CULTURE

The third leg is greed. When I travel outside the country, I am always struck by how greedy we are as a nation. We soak up a hugely disproportionate share of the world's resources. We live in a culture that is built around consuming, and most of that consumption is for things we don't need.

Too often our attitude is to reward the rich and let the rest take care of themselves. While there is a vast gulf in our country between those who have and those who don't, there is even a greater gulf between our Third World neighbors and ourselves. And we wonder why a lot of the rest of the world doesn't like us. Maybe it is because when we want something, we take it. And we don't always share well or play well with others.

As taxes have been reduced we have seen a decline in social services that support those who are the least among us. This has been reflected directly on to education where most states have cut their budgets for schools. Fortunately, while we are affected by greed, I don't see greed being at the heart of the work of most school folks. If you were aspiring to greed, you would have chosen an occupation that would have allowed more wealth accrual. But we can be greedy in other ways. We can pursue our own careers, while not helping others up. We can take care of our district, while the one next door goes begging. We can look out for No. 1 without caring for the other 99.

If we want to dismantle the axis of evil, we have to start at home. Our country needs to re-examine its priorities and behaviors to make sure we are not behaving in ways that create fear, arrogance, and greed. We have to catch ourselves in mid strut and tone it down. And as leaders, we have to look in the mirror each morning to make sure we aren't becoming that which we most despise.

9

ON BECOMING A
HOPE PUSHER

When my children were young, one of them asked me, "Daddy, what does a superintendent do?"

Tough call. I started talking about all the responsibilities that I had—taking care of the buildings, hiring the principals and teachers, and making sure the classrooms have books and materials. Her cute little eyes started glazing over.

Then I mentioned calling school off for snow days and that registered big time. As my kids got older they weren't so happy to be the superintendent's kids because of that. It seems I never closed school often enough as far as they were concerned, and they had to hear about it from their friends. Being the superintendent's kid was the kid equivalent of having leprosy.

Now, as I was explaining to my child what I did, I was technically right but really quite wrong. It wasn't about the stuff of the work that was important. It was about the relationships and the hopes and dreams that I instilled in others. That was my true vocation.

LIBERATING OTHERS

Leading is always people work. And educational leadership is even more people centered than other callings. I am always amazed that as leaders we are constantly trying to figure out what structures and frames we can create to make an organization move where we feel it should go. If we thought about it, we would soon realize that since we are really talking about people you can't structure and frame the human spirit. You can't even contain it. Nor should you.

This has become particularly obvious as superintendents have struggled to find the right course on implementing No Child Left Behind. While the emphasis on accountability and achievement is appropriate, superintendents must find ways of preserving the humanity of those engaged in the learning process. It is important to count how well kids are doing, but it is even more important to make sure that what we are doing to them counts where it counts—in their long-term success and in their human spirit.

Leadership is about liberation. It is about taking lids off, turning lights on, and getting out of the way. Leaders have to be the source of possibility in their organizations—"hope pushers" if you will. Certainly you have to help your people chart the course for their own liberation, but being a leader of people is part inspiration, part cheer-leader, and part referee. You make the future possible. You support their getting there, and occasionally you provide the adult supervision to sort out the bumps and collisions that are inevitable in a human organization.

I have been struck lately in conversations with school leaders how often the term "hope" turns up. It seems more precious than a unanimous school board. One of my staffers mentioned the other day that on a recent visit to Europe she had heard a commentator say the difference between America and Europe was that Europeans didn't believe they could change anything and yet they were hopeful. Americans believe they can change everything and yet they are hopeless. Now I don't know how true that is, but what I do know is that hope is rooted in the belief that you can change things, that you can make the world a better place.

I enjoy engaging school leaders in the question of why they entered the profession. Almost without exception they say because they believed they could make a difference. That is hope at its core—making a difference, making things better. Making the world a kinder and gentler place to dream dreams and pursue possibilities.

In a recent discussion with John Goodlad, we were talking about the superintendency and John posited that superintendents must be the intellectual leaders in their community. By that he meant that they needed to be the most curious and most thoughtful folks around. They should read widely, have multiple interests, and be willing to look behind the obvious and then share that urge to learn with others.

I agreed with John, but I added that they also needed to be the moral leaders in their community. By that I didn't mean they should be leading the singing of "Bless Be the Tie That Binds." But they do need to understand that there is a tie that binds their people to each other and the leader's job is to make sure that tie is maintained and strengthened. The strands that create that tie are made up of hope and maybe even dreams.

BEYOND OPTIMISM

Optimism and hope differ. I seem to be one of those people who possess natural optimism. No matter how much horse manure is around, I am always looking for the pony. But frankly, optimists can get on your nerves. We can be annoying. We're always humming, "The sun will come up tomorrow," but we rarely consider the possibility of sunburn. More than optimism is needed. Optimists can have their hearts broken because they think the world is more benign than it sometimes is. It is necessary for a leader to move beyond optimism to hope.

Optimists think things will get better. People of hope know they will get better, perhaps not quickly or easily, but they know it will happen because while the world is not always benign—it is always good. And goodness always will win out in the end. So, in addition to being intellectual leaders and moral leaders, we have to be hopeful leaders, not so much for ourselves but for those around us. We have to know that even if the sun comes up tomorrow all covered with clouds, that its warmth and light is still available and certainly preferable to the darkness of the night.

So when your child or grandchild asks you what you do—say that you are a source of light and possibility to others. Not a bad calling.

This essay received a bronze award in 2005 from the American Society of Business Publication Editors, Central-Southeast Region.

10

A VIEW FROM
THE TOP

There is a Randy Newman song called "It's Lonely at the Top." Listening to that song always reminds me of how it felt in the years I spent in the superintendency. I once said that superintendents make the Maytag repairman look like a party animal. The very nature of the job is one of splendid isolation.

It always has been curious to me to see how so many extroverted, gregarious folks should happen to choose a profession that cuts them off from the very essence of their humanity. It is lonely at the top.

When you think about it, very few jobs are done singly. Most people work with others and have peers who share job descriptions and responsibility. The irony of the superintendency is that while it is carried out by a person whose job most others don't understand or even care about, its effectiveness is totally dependent upon what others do. A large problem occurs when a gap exists between the leader and those being led.

SHOWING EMPATHY

I was once talking with a group of teachers and they complained that I couldn't possibly understand their issues because it had been so long since I had been in a classroom. I acknowledged they had a point, but I went on to suggest to them that at least I had been in a

classroom at one time in my life; they had never been a superintendent and couldn't possibly understand things from my perspective.

The lesson here for leaders is that you can only see the world
clearly when looking through another's eyes. It is the old adage
that to understand someone you have to walk in his shoes.
Superintendents have to be willing to spend most of their days trying on other folks' loafers and looking out through others' eyes. Only
then can you begin to lead others by demonstrating to them you are
capable of understanding their needs. People will only entrust their
hearts to you when they feel they can trust you with them. If a leader
wants to be trusted, then he or she must demonstrate empathy.

I always have been fascinated with mountain climbers—not that
I would ever want to be one myself. But you have to be curious
about a mentality that drives someone to spend days of struggle at
risk of life and limb to climb a mountain that could easily be flown
over in several seconds.

We all have seen pictures of the lone climber who mounts that
one last step to the summit and surveys a landscape that stretches
below in all directions. That climber knows how truly lonely it can be
at the top, but she also understands how magnificent the scenery can
be. And she knows the view was made possible by the test. It is only
through testing that any of us can feel the sense of accomplishment.

Leadership is about taking the risk to enjoy the rewards. Not
everyone is willing to do that, but that is what makes a leader a
leader. And it is good to remember that while the photo opportunity
is of the lonely climber who got to the summit, he or she didn't get
there alone. Mountains are scaled by teams.

I often have joked that I have a real problem crossing bridges.
I get very "white knuckled" when I have to drive across a bridge. My
friends tell me I have a phobia about it. I beg to differ. Phobias are
irrational fears, and there is nothing irrational about being afraid to
cross a bridge because bridges take you from what you know to what
you don't know. They take you from a place of comfort to a place of
possible discomfort. Yet that is what education is about and that is
what leadership is about—building bridges and escorting people
across them to unknown territory.

Albert Einstein once said teachers are messengers from the past
and escorts to the future. And so are leaders. Leaders open new
worlds to people and they understand that exploration is a lonely
business. But bridges are built by crews and exploration is typically
undertaken by expeditions.

Group Solidarity

The thing we have to keep in mind is that while our work is lonely, it is a mutually dependent activity. While we know that no one really knows or understands our work, our task is to create a sense of mutuality and an understanding that all things are connected. And to do that we must be connected.

A recent series of TV commercials for AARP focused on individuals doing something of great impact. One featured a housewife calling the president and talking him into fixing Social Security and another showed a lady bringing in a group of CEOs to fix the health care crisis. The tag line was, "If we could do it alone, we wouldn't need AARP." I have used that thought in encouraging folks to belong to AASA, but it is also a powerful idea for any leader. If we could do it alone, we wouldn't need each other.

It sometimes can be a lonely world and there is little doubt we have chosen a lonely profession. But that doesn't mean we have to be alone. We have to use our humanity to connect to those we work with. And we have to be grateful for the gift we have been given to be leaders.

We can make the world a better place. That is a powerful mission. So it is lonely at the top, but that is where you get the best view.

This essay received a bronze award in 2005 from the American Society of Business Publication Editors, Central-Southeast Region.

11

LIFE'S LESSONS FROM
MY DOG HOLLY

Shortly after my mother passed away last summer I realized my life had truly changed. She left me her dog. Now, giving me a dog is cruel and unusual punishment—for the dog. Let's just say my lifestyle and travel schedule doesn't easily accommodate an ongoing responsibility. But you know what? It's been a great learning experience for me. And from it I have developed some lessons for leaders.

Lesson No. 1: Every walk is a new walk.

I take Holly for a walk twice a day near my home. Because I live in an urban area I have to take her pretty much the same route each time to maximize the available grass. What I find fascinating is that she acts like she has never walked that way before. Every sight and smell is brand new and endlessly intriguing to her.

As leaders we can sometimes become bored with our activities and come to think we have seen it all before. The truth is, we haven't. There is a teaching from Zen that you can never step in the same river twice. The world is constantly changing and if you don't accept that, you will miss the nuances of change. You have to be open to new sights and smells, even on a familiar path.

A corollary to this is the teaching from Tom Peters and Robert Waterman that you need to manage by walking around. But while you're walking, be careful where you step. Keep your eyes open and your nose ready—which leads to the next lesson.

SENSORY SKILLS

Lesson No. 2: You have to smell around to enjoy things.

I can't get over how much that dog likes to sniff around. No good smell goes undetected. Now personally, I wouldn't want to smell some of the stuff she smells, but it seems irresistible to her. Most of the time I just walk past things. Holly digs down and really examines them at a very sensory level. How many leaders really get to know their environments the way a dog does? Few I would suspect.

Lesson No. 3: Dogs are always glad to see you.

It doesn't much matter what is going on, when I come home Holly races to the door to say hello and to inquire about her walk. I might have had a bad day, been overcome with controversy and conflict or whatever, but there is Holly just glad to see me. We read a lot about unconditional love, but we don't see a lot of it. Yet the task of leaders is to give their people the kind of loyalty and concern that a dog shows everyday. One of our politicians once observed that if you want someone in Washington to like you, get a dog. He was right.

Lesson No. 4: Dogs don't wear watches.

When I take Holly for her walks I am usually in a hurry—running late, needing to get to my next task or whatever. She couldn't care less. It just doesn't matter to her. I realized that is because she doesn't wear a watch. She doesn't know what time it is. Dogs are in the moment. They don't care what happened yesterday. They aren't worrying about tomorrow. They are focused on the now. So should we be.

Lesson No. 5: Dogs eat a little, sleep a little, and enjoy themselves.

We hear a lot about the need for balance in our lives. I have written about it. (I write better than I act on this topic!) Most of us know more about this than we do. Dogs don't know that much—they just do it. They eat when they get hungry, sleep when they get tired, and play with their toys when they need entertainment.

Lesson No. 6: Dogs wag their tail to show their intentions.

When my dog approaches another dog, she wags her tail to show she is friendly. I sometimes think it is unfortunate we don't have a tail to wag to show our friendly intentions. We do bare our teeth at each other, but most of the time we could avoid problems by being friendlier to each other.

Lesson No. 7: Dogs don't clean up their messes.

I also have learned some negative lessons from Holly. First of all, dogs don't clean up after themselves—I have to do that. Leaders not only have to clean up their own messes, they have to clean up other people's messes. While dogs are dependent, leaders must take responsibility for their lives and for those around them.

CLARIFYING NEEDS

Lesson No. 8: Dogs can't communicate as clearly as humans.

Despite the fact that Holly is pretty smart and does a lot of interesting things, I have realized that she has yet to really tell me what she needs or even what she is thinking about. She gives me clues through looks and barks, but I find her lack of clarity extremely frustrating. It would be so much better if instead of pulling back on the leash, she would just say, "Hey, interesting smell here, wait up." I am left trying to interpret her silence. Leaders must be sure they're communicating effectively to maximize results.

Lesson No. 9: Dogs can't tell the difference between a street and a sidewalk.

In Holly's case the difference amounts to going after a big dog or being fearful of a small one. The fact is leadership can be dangerous and risky. It is good to know what to fear and where safety lies. And sometimes it is just good to curl up in a warm spot and chew on something.

(Author's epilogue: A few weeks after I wrote this, Holly got very ill and passed away. It took me back to the thought on unconditional love. When you receive it, enjoy it while it lasts. And it wouldn't hurt to give it to others.)

SECTION II

NEW ROLE: SUPERINTENDENT OF EDUCATION

12

GETTING IT RIGHT

Have you ever noticed that everyone wants something from you? Usually in our work this involves answers, resources, or solutions. I often joke that if I ever write a book on the superintendency (and watch out, after I retire I might just have the time to do so), I would call it, *"What Are You Going to Do About It?"* That question seemed to be the one I always got when I was a superintendent.

Superintendents are the answer people. They are the Mr. or Mrs. "Fix-its." They are asked to just make it all better. They are asked to take away the pain of others when that very act can cause them pain.

As leaders, we may get caught up responding to someone else's agenda—taking care of their needs, doing their bidding. This means it is often hard for us to do what we know we need to do. In fact, since we are always responding instead of thinking, we might not even know what we need to do. How can we think when we are so busy doing?

A Few Clues

This demand for action so central to our work is one thing that makes us less effective. Sometimes the best way to move forward is to step back. Reflective practice is at the heart of effective leadership. Great leaders not only do the right things, they know *why* they are doing them—otherwise you are just pulling the handle of the slot machine and hoping for the best.

So what is it we should do? The lead article in the February 2008 issue of *The School Administrator* gives us some clues. It features a conversation between authors Tom Friedman and Dan Pink on the challenges facing our world and the implications for educators and administrators. Friedman's pitch, which has been misinterpreted by many to say that we must produce more engineers and scientists to compete with India and China, is that we must produce more creative people, including scientists and engineers.

That has been my tune for several years. America's greatest strength historically has been our ability to innovate and create. Friedman and Pink say yes, we need to do even more of that in the future. And we need to do so with a spirit that allows children to use both sides of their brains and to be in touch with their whole selves. Friedman calls the American ability to integrate art, music, and literature with the hard sciences the "secret sauce" that America has that other countries do not.

One of the greatest dangers of our emphasis on high-stakes testing, standards, and accountability is that the secret sauce is being left off the meal. We are so focused on those things that can be counted we are leaving out those things that count. We are leading in a world that is not "either/or" but it is "and." We need rigorous learning *and* a breadth of curriculum. We need students to know facts *and* to have a sense of fancy and fantasy. We need students who can do what our politicians seem unable to do—to hold more than one complex idea in their minds at one time, to allow for the notion that things that seem contradictory or unrelated might just be able to reside together and be necessary. To borrow Friedman's book title, the world might just be flat and round at the same time.

How do we as leaders help teachers and our communities come to understand that education must be about the whole child and the whole mind? How do we slow our world down long enough to know what are the right things we should be doing? That is the real challenge for today's leaders. While I have certainly supported the idea of data-driven decision making, it is good to remember that it is not a lack of data we suffer from. It is a lack of wisdom.

TOUCHING LIVES

It always has seemed a great irony to me as educators whose jobs it is to promote thought and learning, we find ourselves so strapped for time we don't think and learn ourselves. It is not that superintendents read too little—we read too much of the wrong things. It is reading that is fragmented and piecemeal and does not lead to wisdom. It is not that we don't think—it is that we are forced to spend so much time thinking about the wrong things. Memos and letters of complaint might inform us, but I doubt if they make us wiser. We must spend more time in reflection and in thinking deeply about what we ought to be doing and what the important issues of our work are.

Friedman says in his discussion with Pink that we need more "yes but-ers" in the system. I think that is the essence of the role of superintendents. We have to be the ones who say yes to things—to turn the lights on. If we are the "no-ers" in the system, we can never be the knowers. We have to empower folks around us to seek new possibilities.

Friedman also says that superintendents need to "know what you believe and stick with it." You have to be the compass for those around you—letting them know where true north lies. He reminds us it is about standing our ground. I would remind us it is also about knowing the ground you are standing on.

Some of that ground must be about what the right kind of education is needed—education that integrates learning and that emphasizes the connections between things and people. It must be education that speaks to their whole minds.

And we can't lose sight of the very essence of what we do. We are alchemists. We touch people and make them something else. Education is, at its core, the task of taking something of no apparent worth and making something priceless out of it. We have the opportunity, through our caring and our wisdom, to enhance the lives of others, to help them be something they are not—to spin straw into gold.

13

REVENGE OF
THE BLOB

When I was a young superintendent, I prayed for business leaders and politicians to pay more attention to education.

If we could find a way to get the titans of industry, the governors, the legislators, the Congress, and maybe even the president to focus more on education, we could really make progress. And have they ever! This is an example of the need to be careful what you pray for because you might get it.

In fact, my praying led to my feeling of being preyed upon by these very same groups. What we got first was the *A Nation at Risk* report that told us we were experiencing a "rising tide of mediocrity" in our schools, and our nation was at risk if we didn't improve schools dramatically. That report was followed by dozens of others blaming the schools for one shortcoming or another.

According to critics, school leaders were no longer leaders—they were the "blob," as Secretary of Education William Bennett put it. In the midst of all the hysteria, America reemerged as the No. 1 economic and military power, but no one came to thank me for making America great again.

TRIVIAL APPROACH

Instead we got an era of "amateur school reform." If the professional leaders couldn't lead, then business folks and politicians would do it. Sadly, their main school expertise was achieved by their once attending school. Meanwhile, school leaders have been marginalized and blamed as part of the problem rather than the solution.

Even a recent study by the "New" Commission on Skills of the American Workforce called "Tough Choices or Tough Times" continues the attack saying, we don't need professional leaders. The commission suggests that leadership of schools should be handled by independent outside contractors. District offices would write and manage contracts with the operators of these schools. This is the compliance model taken to its ultimate conclusion. I was struck once again by the assumption that leadership just doesn't matter.

How is it that leadership matters so much in every other realm of endeavor but not in schools? Well, there is mounting evidence that the critics of school leaders are just dead wrong. Leadership in schools and school districts matters, just as it does in business or even on commissions that release widely publicized reports. And it is time for the "blob" to exact its revenge on those who question the usefulness of leadership at the local level.

COMPREHENSIVE ANALYSIS

Notable in the midst of all this is a report released by the Mid-continent Research for Education and Learning laboratory coauthored by Tim Waters and Robert Marzano. They studied all the major quantitative research available on student achievement and leadership.

In the end, they found superintendent leadership matters—a lot. Their study greatly exceeded the threshold for validity and what they found was that not all leadership mattered, but certain activities enacted by the superintendent mattered a great deal to the outcome of improving student achievement.

They found that when the superintendent (1) involves board and principals in the goal-setting process; (2) provides autonomy to principals to lead within the alignment on district goals and uses resources for professional development; (3) has a board that supports district goals; (4) dedicates the necessary resources for professional development to achieve district goals; (5) monitors and evaluates implementation of the district instructional program; and (6) makes certain that goals for student achievement and instructional programs are adopted and based on relevant research, the outcome is remarkable. Student achievement goes up by as much as 10 percent. One unanticipated finding of the study was that stability in leadership also matters. Changing superintendents has negative consequences on student achievement.

A BREED APART

Good news also emerged from a recent study on the superintendency conducted by AASA. Despite the lack of respect afforded the position nationally and the pressures on it, most people doing the job are finding satisfaction in it. Nearly 9 out of 10 would choose the profession again and more than 90 percent believe they are effective and are satisfied with the job.

Superintendents, as a breed, seem to be very high-minded. They went into the job, not for perks, but for the opportunity to serve. Having a greater impact on student achievement was the No. 1 reason for entering the role, according to the survey

What the McREL and AASA studies show is that superintendents became superintendents to make a difference, particularly in improving the learning outcomes for children. And when they focus on that and collaborate with boards of education and principals around that goal, good things happen in their districts.

We know our value. We always have known it. Now the studies show that leaders matter and district leadership really matters. District leaders who operate from a command-and-control perspective or who go to the opposite extreme by choosing to let others lead will not be successful. Those who have a servant leader bias and who can focus on what is really important will make a difference.

It is time for the members of blob to rise out of the swamp of disrespect and assert ourselves. Can I get a roar out there?

14

NEARLY FAMOUS

Shortly after my arrival as the new superintendent in Tucson, Arizona, with all the attendant media fanfare given to the new "Piñata in Chief," I was invited to one of my staff member's homes for dinner. I rang the bell and his young son opened the door. He took a hard look at me, his eyes brightened and he said, "Oh, I know you—you're nearly famous."

It later struck me how right he was. That is the category in which most superintendents find themselves—nearly famous. You're somebody, but people just aren't sure who.

Being the superintendent in a town with two daily newspapers, four TV stations, and not much to focus on except the university athletic programs and local schools, I got all sorts of experience finding out what it felt like to be nearly famous. It was always a bit crazy to walk through the aisles of Costco and hear people discussing me as if I wasn't there. I think because they had seen me on television, they assumed I was still in the little box and couldn't hear what they had to say. Or I would be in a restaurant with friends and realize all the other diners around us were leaning toward us like we were E. F. Hutton because they were curious what the superintendent might be discussing.

Other times people would look at me with a glimmer of recognition, knowing I was someone, but they just weren't sure who. Several asked which news show I was on. "All of them" was my answer. Once a lady asked me if anyone had ever told me I looked a lot like Paul Houston. I told her the truth: "No, no one has ever told me that before."

FREE COUNSEL

When I was superintendent in the small town of Princeton, New Jersey, I didn't get the media exposure, but I was very big in the checkout line of the supermarket or on the sidewalk after church on Sunday. Everyone had a question or more often an opinion. I used to observe I had the easiest job in town because everyone knew what I should do and was happy to tell me. I just could never get them to speak with one voice. Superintendents get lots of free advice, but sorting it all out can be a challenge.

The truth is that the job we have chosen for ourselves is certainly more than running an organization. We are the public face on a complex and often misunderstood institution, and we have to find ways of feeling comfortable playing that role. In many ways we also serve as the lightning rod for the public's disappointments and dissatisfaction. When things are going well, it is the teachers and principals who are getting it done. When things aren't going well, a search party is formed with the superintendent in the crosshairs. And while that may not feel fair, it strikes me that it is pretty much the way it should be.

Good leadership should focus outward and illuminate those doing the work. It should never be about you. It should always be about them. When I first became a superintendent I used to get a chuckle (and truth be known a bit of a thrill) walking into a meeting and hearing people say, "Oh, Mr. Superintendent" or "The superintendent is here, let's see what he says about that." It didn't take me long to realize that the focus I was getting cuts both ways. Yes, I was in a position that people looked up to and that had influence, but I was also the one easily blamed if things didn't go right or who was held accountable for what needed to happen next.

Being "Mr. Superintendent" wasn't always all it was cracked up to be. But the real work I did was to keep the pressure off the people doing the business of educating. I realized my job was to be the tent pole in that little circus, and I had to keep the canvas from smothering the performers. It was an important job, but sometimes one that made me nearly famous in ways I didn't particularly enjoy.

CONVERSATION STARTER

I have heard people say that superintendents are all extroverts. I am not sure that is true, but you better do a pretty good job of faking "extrovertism" if you hope to succeed.

However, I think the best way to look at the job is that of being a catalytic converter. You are a catalyst whose presence, vision, energy, and insight can help jumpstart the conversation and move others to mountaintops they didn't know they could climb. You also must convert the work and the language into actions that the community understands and can support.

I have observed that being the superintendent is like being the dolphin trainer at Sea World. You have to ride on the backs of two dolphins, with a foot on each. In the case of the superintendent, one dolphin is the staff and the other is the community. You have to keep a balance between the two or you'll fall off your dolphin.

The job of superintendent is both internal and external. You have to use your position to help the staff move forward, and you have to engage and enlist the community in supporting the job. Basically, you have to help the staff understand they are not as good as they think and the community to understand the staff is better than they think. That is where you can use the "fame" you have been given.

Superintendents are among the most influential people in their communities. There is a reason why they are nearly famous. While the job may not carry all the respect it once had, it is still one that makes a difference in the lives of children and the future of the community. Superintendents must be the intellectual and moral leaders in their communities. They can focus the conversation on the right things and can call people to a higher place. While you may be only nearly famous, you have the opportunity to be wholly critical to the future.

15

A CRITICAL POSITION IN CRITICAL CONDITION

The history of the school superintendency has been a fitful journey from manager to leader. The role has evolved from an ad hoc response to local needs for school management to leading a complex community learning enterprise. It is a position that is widely influential but narrowly understood.

One must admit that today, if we were part of the medical profession, superintendents would be listed in critical condition. We have political leaders who want to reduce the number of superintendents or lower their pay. We have others who feel that anyone can be a superintendent: The irony is that at the very time when teaching and learning are central to the work, boards of education are hiring leaders who know nothing about either.

Other politicians want to work around superintendents or to scapegoat superintendents for all the problems of education—many of which emanate from the failures of these very same politicians. We see educational amateurs in the corporate and political world tell the professionals what to do, how to do it, and what will happen if they don't do it. Even though these amateurs lack the insight even to know what they don't know, they have the power and they are calling the tunes.

The superintendency has become a job with lots of accountability but limited authority and one that many have called the most complex job in America. Little wonder there is a shortage in those willing to tackle it.

BRIDGE BUILDERS

Yet there is another side to the story. There are thousands of professional educators who get up every morning and go to their jobs as superintendents, dedicated to creating a brighter future for children. They find ways to transform the intrusion of government mandates into lemonade. They work past the poverty of some of their students to create safe havens for children.

Superintendents protect America. Our forefathers were wise enough to create a system of public education in this country that allows a diverse and disparate people to come to a common setting to learn to set aside their differences and live together as one nation. And this institution was so vital it would be paid for by all our citizens because each would have a stake in its success.

It is ironic to me that when the 9/11 Commission issued its report, it called for the creation of public schools in the Middle East to allow people seeking to live more democratically a way to get past the narrow teachings of the jihadists. You can't have a modern democracy without a joint agreement by its citizens that they will put aside their differences and personal desires for the good of the whole. For democracy to thrive, public education must survive.

Yet we know there are those who would dismantle the public education system to replace it with their private vision. Will we destroy the one institution in our country designed to bring people to a sense of common good? And can that common good emerge from narrow self-interest?

Superintendents are engaged in a battle of competing visions of a future America. One would serve private interests through choice and by starving the public institutions of the resources necessary for success. The other would see that we are all in this together and we have a compact with each other and a common destiny to fulfill.

In the midst of this battle stand the superintendents who must maintain a steady course, while being able to moderate and mediate the shifting political pressures. Although it is important to find common ground inside the system, it is also important to confront those from outside who would threaten these institutions.

Martin Luther King once said, "We are caught in an inescapable network of mutuality, tied into a single garment of destiny and that what affects one directly, affects all indirectly." I am reminded of a professor I once heard who observed that if you drain the Pacific Ocean, you would find that all the islands are connected. Once you get past the surface of things that seem to show we are on separate islands, if you go deep enough, all are one. Standing up for public education is about protecting that little boat that we share on that big ocean that can take us from where we are to where our dreams might lead us.

THE RIGHT CHOICE

Preserving possibilities for children requires leadership. And that leadership is a critical condition for success. Evidence is emerging that when one tries to find the critical variable in school reform, it is the superintendent. While the educational journey takes place in the classroom and school, the trip is planned, the fuel acquired, and the steering done in the superintendent's office. Good superintendents are the critical condition for system success.

The work of the superintendent is to be a warrior for justice, a healer for those in pain, and a lighthouse keeper to help folks find their way. The work is vital to the future of democracy. It requires us to reach the broader community in new and creative ways. Our role is that of transformative leaders who must bring out the best in those around us. We are dream merchants and civic sailors.

Yes, superintendents are in the critical position to create the conditions for a successful future. In one of the Harry Potter movies, Headmaster Dumbledore tells Harry that "dark days are ahead—and we will be faced with the choice between that which is easy and that which is right."

Superintendents, by choosing the work we do, have already made that choice. We chose to do the right and not the easy. As we face an uncertain future, we must continue to lead by doing the right thing.

16

ON THE
PENGUIN MARCH
THROUGH LIFE

In the midst of a very hot summer I saw a very cool movie, *The March of the Penguins*. I had heard it was unique in its charm, humor, and emotion. Also, because I had traveled to Antarctica just months earlier, I wanted a chance to revisit the experience.

Besides that, when it is 100 degrees outside, watching snow and ice for a couple of hours sounds like a great idea. And it was, but the movie isn't just about penguins, it is about love and sacrifice, and I saw much of our work in it.

The movie is more stuffed with metaphors than a penguin after a two-week eating frenzy. There is something about penguins that captures our imagination. Perhaps it is because they remind us of ourselves with their little penguin tuxedos and their loopy, comical gait. In fact, the movie opens with a long shot of a line of something walking across the ice. Is it a row of people?

No, it is a line of emperor penguins beginning their trek across the ice of the South Pole from their feeding area in the ocean to their breeding grounds 70 miles inland. It is a march they will repeat several times during the course of the winter. And there is nothing more daunting than the Antarctic winter—70 degrees below zero and winds of 100 miles an hour. It makes snow days look rather pedestrian.

Emperor penguins must fill their bellies with food for they go months between meals. They return to the breeding grounds, where they were born, to mate, lay eggs, and raise their babies. It is hard to imagine a more difficult place or time for this. It is the most inhospitable part of a vacant and savage continent and they carry this out in winter.

COLLABORATIVE BEHAVIOR

As I watched them conduct their mission I naturally thought of us and our work. We have chosen a role that is difficult and dangerous and some would say foolish. Yet, like the emperor penguins, we see to our responsibilities and do what must be done to allow the next generation to have its chance.

One of the powerful lessons from the movie is the fact that those who fall behind or seek to go it alone fail to survive. They disappear into the frozen landscape. It is only through collaborative behavior between the males and females, and ultimately among the males themselves, that survival is possible among penguins; it is the male who tends to the egg and the hatchling while the female goes back to the ocean for food.

As the winter storms roar around them, the males must huddle together, each taking a turn on the outside where the wind blows strongest, and then later a turn in the middle of the scrum where there is the most protection from the cold. Adult males must constantly balance their eggs on the feet, tucked under their bellies for warmth. Eventually the female will return with food for the chick, allowing the male to go back to the ocean to feed.

One of the things I found most interesting about all this is that only the penguins that are bringing forth the next generation participate in this. The others stay happily at sea, eating and living an easier life. It seems to me that the humans who choose to look after the young face the same kind of daunting challenge. In many ways, I think the times we are in now are our own version of a winter of extremes. But after winter comes spring and life moves forward.

All this led me to remember my own penguin adventures in Antarctica. I spent hours when we were ashore watching them. Two moments stand out. The first involved a lone penguin making his way back to the nest. I imagined him as a school superintendent. He hopped off a rock right into the middle of a major mud puddle. Oh the memories that brought back! As a superintendent, I had stepped in the mud many a time myself. What to do? What to do?

He was already up to his little penguin bottom in mud so he chose to move forward, slopping through the mud, still trying to get home. Just as when we get stuck, we have only one choice. We're already dirty. We may as well move forward and complete the journey. Finally he got near the nest only to be sent packing by the spouse who set off a horrendous squawk of "penguinese" that must have meant, "You don't think you are going to track all over my nice nest with those muddy feet, do you?" My boy stopped for a few seconds, shrugged, and turned away. The lesson here is that sometimes you can't even go home again even after a hard day in the mud—or perhaps the message is you shouldn't take your mud home with you.

FUNDAMENTAL DECISIONS

The other moment came watching a line of hundreds of penguins marching along the shore in single file. The first penguin in line came to a large rock. He hopped up on the rock and stopped, and the whole line stopped behind him. He was deciding whether he should dive. For the sea is home to the krill, which is the major source of food for the penguin, but it is also where the leopard seals live, and penguins are the major source of food to the leopard seal.

So really the leader was making a life or death decision. Food? Leopard seals? Leopard seals? Food? What to do? While he debated, none of the other penguins broke ranks. They waited for the leader to decide the next move.

He paused for at least five minutes and finally dived off the rock and into the water. And after him came each penguin in turn, following his lead and moving toward life. The roles we play can have tremendous implications—not just for ourselves but for those who follow our lead. We must pause and think, be willing to risk the mud or the leopard seals, but ultimately we must make a choice that allows life to move forward. We are all on a penguin march toward our possibilities, moving through the cold night so that we can find the spring.

17

WHO YOU GONNA CALL?

A few years ago the theme song for a popular movie *Ghostbusters* raised the question that when there was something strange in your neighborhood, "Who you gonna call?" The answer, of course, was Ghostbusters.

The answer to the question of who you're going to call when trouble happens in a school community is always the same—the superintendent. I have joked if I ever write a book on the superintendency I'm going to call it, *What Are You Going to Do About It?* The reality is that superintendents are always the spear point when trouble erupts.

Many players comprise the education mix, from school board members to classroom teachers and principals. If school boards are doing their jobs properly, they are setting policy, approving goals, and auditing progress. They are not doing the day-to-day work of implementation.

Likewise teachers and principals are the "boots on the ground," to borrow a current term. They are on the front lines doing the grunt work of making progress on a daily basis. But when the unexpected arises and problems present themselves, it is the superintendent who must pull together all the pieces and make things happen up and down the line.

AT THE FOREFRONT

That is why, after the recent disasters of Hurricanes Katrina and Rita, it was the superintendents who stepped up. Across the country, hundreds of superintendents galvanized their school districts to receive displaced students. They helped welcome them and make them and their families feel at home in a strange place. They worked with their communities to pull together resources, and they organized their systems to provide the educational, psychological, and, in many cases, the logistical help the children and families needed. No one asked, "What's in it for me?" or even whether extra resources would be forthcoming.

In the directly affected areas, superintendents set aside their own personal issues and family crises. Their focus was how to get their schools back on line so the children who remained or who returned could continue their learning. In times of crises, America produces thousands of heroes and heroines, and numbered among them are the many superintendents who stood firm in a strong wind and pulled it together for the children.

The reality now remains that, after the initial response is winding down, the long-range response that will be needed is staggering. Literally hundreds of schools are demolished and must be replaced. Hundreds of others need massive renovation. Yet, in these same communities, the tax bases that would normally be called upon to build schools no longer exist. And the taxpayers have no jobs to go to and no money to pay taxes. Teachers have been displaced and many may not return to their original districts. The infrastructure of the systems must be re-established and, in many cases rebuilt. That is why AASA has called for more than $10 billion in school reconstruction money to be supplied through federal sources.

Meanwhile, those superintendents who selflessly reached out to embrace the evacuated children will face the harsh reality that their local and state sources of money for resident children will not cover the costs of the additional flood of children many are now serving. From where will those resources come? Again, AASA has proposed a one-year federal allotment for each child accepted equal to the annual per-pupil cost.

TROUBLED WATERS

Other problems are unresolved. Flexibility will be needed in handling these children. We hope the Department of Education will stand behind its pledge to ensure no school district will be penalized under provisions of the No Child Left Behind Act because it opened its doors to displaced and traumatized children. NCLB's accountability standards should take into account that these children may fail to make adequate yearly progress. Likewise, we hope districts will not be subject to lawsuits because they failed to meet the timelines for producing individual education plans under IDEA for children who may have such a plan under 10 feet of water in Louisiana or Mississippi.

At the time of publication, the U.S. Secretary of Education has not said whether she will be flexible when it comes to regulations that cover homeless children. The reality is that thus far, Washington bureaucracy in all areas has been leaden and shown a remarkable insensitivity to the issues created by Katrina and Rita. Shouldn't educators' good intentions be trusted? When hundreds of thousands of children are homeless, the Department will, we hope, realize that it does not make sense to address problems on a case-by-case basis.

The reality is the flood waters of Katrina and Rita are but the first of the waves of trouble facing education across the region and country. President Bush has vowed to rebuild the region and make it better than before. He also acknowledged the role that extreme poverty played in the victimization of so many and said that also needs to be addressed. But I would remind the president that the poor are with us in every region and the public schools are the epicenter of dealing with so many who have been left behind.

The good news in all this troubled water is that superintendents will be doing what they always do—standing in the gap to provide leadership, vision, and compassion. Superintendents aren't bureaucrats, even though the pressure of the last few years has made them number crunchers. Superintendents aren't just the "say no" people who stop parents, teachers, and children from having their individual way. They are the village builders who mediate the injustices created by an unfair system and the collaborators who bring the pieces together. They are truly the ghostbusters who, in good times and bad, clear the air and make things safe. Who you gonna call? We all know the answer to that one.

18

BUILDING
FIELDS OF DREAMS

I never can visit Iowa without thinking of one of my movie favorites, *Field of Dreams*. Last summer, as I was flying into Des Moines, I was looking out of the window enjoying the lush landscape of varied hues of green, some so deep they seemed blue. I kept hearing the words of Shoeless Joe Jackson asking the Kevin Costner character, Ray Kinsella, if the baseball field he was standing in was heaven. Ray replied, "No, this is Iowa."

Iowans like that line too and you see it posted on T-shirts and mugs. Coming from a state that promoted itself as "Almost Heaven, West Virginia," I understand the pride involved. Flying in on that summer evening, it was also easy to see why Shoeless Joe was confused.

But I can never think of *Field of Dreams* without thinking about the work we do. The movie is filled with the themes that I believe make being an educator so powerful—dreams, hopes, redemption, connection, and perseverance. It was a movie that made us feel good by reminding us of what is best about ourselves. There are times when educators need to remind themselves of the power of their work.

DARK TO LIGHT

It is difficult to reconcile the work of educational leaders as strictly a management issue. So much of what we do deals with the aspirations and dreams of the people we serve. You can't manage dreams; you have to pump them up and let them soar. Deepak Chopra said leaders are the symbolic soul of the groups they lead. But for leaders to "thrive on chaos" they must understand the underlying order, which has a spiritual basis. He pointed out that choosing to lead is "choosing to step out of the darkness." By implication, stepping out of darkness puts us under the lights.

Like many across the world I grew up a fan of John F. Kennedy and the magic he sprinkled on America as its leader. I was particularly taken by his espousing and modeling the line from Hemingway about the need to "exhibit grace under pressure." That is the gold standard for a leader to pursue—an "amazing grace" that allows everyone around you to be better than he or she thinks possible. Leaders must not only exhibit grace, they must dispense it.

But getting back to Ray Kinsella. You recall he was working in the cornfield, minding his own business, when a voice whispers to him, "If you build it, he will come." It's mysterious and unnerving. Yet when you think about it, haven't we all been called to the work that we are doing? Our jobs aren't to raise some corn and make a profit. And while it is blasphemy in today's world of assessment and accountability, it isn't to raise test scores and make AYP (adequate yearly progress) either. Our mission is to build it.

Sometimes we get lost in trying to figure out the "it." You remember Ray needed awhile to figure out that it was a baseball field in the middle of his cornfield. But it wasn't really about the field; it was about the opportunity for redemption, first for Shoeless Joe and his teammates, but ultimately for Ray and his relationship with his father. We all share the need to make things over.

And what an act of faith it was for Ray. By plowing under his corn, he gave up the profits he needed to keep his farm and support his family, and he lost the good opinion of his extended family and neighbors. They thought he was crazy. Have you ever done anything crazy because you were called to do it? Isn't that what leadership often entails? But we must remember Ray did it because he was serving a larger purpose—he was preparing a way, making things ready. It wasn't the field, it was the action to take place on it—a chance to play catch once more with his dad.

HEALING OTHERS

Building anything requires vision, planning, and effort. But it moves quickly from the practical to the spiritual—to build something you also must have faith and you must believe. You have to see it real before it happens.

But building the field just led to the next mission: "Go the distance." For Ray that meant a trip across country. For most of us, it means staying the course, making commitments, and keeping them. Leaders must persevere before they can prevail. Leading isn't just finding the right path. It means staying on it. This requires courage to face the dangers and resilience to recover from the blows.

The final mission given to Ray was to "ease his pain." Leadership is at its core the art of "healership." But leaders don't do the healing. They create the conditions for the people to heal themselves. But first we must do no harm. Sadly, in many organizations we have leaders inflicting pain, rather than easing it.

Ultimately, Ray discovers that while he thought he was doing all these things for others, it was really for himself. In building and going the distance, he was really easing his own pain. The reality is that whatever we do to others, we do to ourselves and whatever we do for others, we do for ourselves. That is the secret perk and peril of being a leader.

As Ray grapples with how he will hold on to his farm, he is urged by his daughter to keep it because people will pay to come and visit. James Earl Jones's character tells Ray they will come and pay because it is money they have but peace they lack. Touching a field of dreams offers the peace they need. Ultimately, our task is to offer a chance for peace to others, and peace is only possible when dreams are there.

At the end of the movie Ray asks his father if there is a heaven and his father tells him, "Yes, it's the place where dreams come true." The real calling and the real payoff for school leaders is that we can create heaven on earth by helping children's dreams come true. That offers us amazing grace.

This essay received a Silver Award in 2006 from the American Society of Business Publication Editors, Central-Southeast Region. It also received an Excellence in Writing award in the National School Public Relations Association's 2006 Publications and Electronic Media Contest.

19

TO LEAD MY TREK, I PICK SCOTTY

I recently arrived home from another trip—late again. The airline lost my luggage—again. Traveling today makes me long for the future promised in *Star Trek*. If you want to be somewhere else, you simply get Scotty to beam you there. You arrive instantaneously— unruffled, unlagged, and with all your stuff.

As we approach the new millennium, much of our attention is focused on the future. I often am involved in discussions with other educational leaders about the future of education. On our worst days, we wonder if there will be a future for public education. On our best days, we become deeply engaged in how we might reshape the world to ensure a better education for our children.

To get where we need to go, we will need to have a vision for what we want, a sense of mission that will shape how we carry out the vision and a deep sense of purpose to ensure that it happens. In essence, we have to be visionaries and missionaries. However, we also have to be a bit like Scotty, an engineer who can design the work and get the ship up to speed.

ENVIABLE CHARACTERS

I am sure someone will try to capture the spirit of *Star Trek* by writing a book called *Captain Kirk on Leadership*. Hasn't each of us

wanted to sit on the bridge and call out, "Warp speed, Mr. Sulu," so
we could see our own enterprise take flight on a journey where no
one has gone before? Haven't we all envied Kirk's coolness and his
bravery? He was a captain in charge.

Or perhaps we have envied Spock's logic (if not his pointy ears)
in the face of disaster and his ability to keep his head when all
around him were losing theirs. Of course, that headiness was coun-
tered by Bones McCoy with deep-seated humanity. However, for me
the key figure aboard the *Enterprise* was always Scotty.

Despite unrealistic expectations and demands, Scotty, who filled
the role of chief engineer, was always ready to get the job done:
"Aye Captain, I'm giving it all that I've got." He would always
figure out how to get a little more power out of the ship or how to
get the force field strong enough to ward off danger or how to get the
rescue party down to the surface. Of all the characters in *Star Trek,*
Scotty comes closer than any to modeling the day-to-day work of
school leaders.

A HEAD AND HEART

The truly visionary leader does not merely give vision to the organization as Kirk did. When you think about it, the crew, by following
Kirk, was always "warping" around the universe from one galaxy to
another. They saw a lot and had great adventures, but I am unclear as
to what they accomplished. Organizations must create their own
sense of vision, their own destination. Visionary leaders are those
who can extract that vision from the organization, articulate it clearly
back to the organization and help all to see their own vision so they
know where they are going and so everyone can get there together.

Mission-driven organizations have a head and a heart—a Spock
and a Bones. It requires both to succeed. A brain without a heart is
sterile. A heart without a head is random. Spock lacked humor.
Bones lacked direction. Both were great guys, but I would not want
to be stranded on a distant planet with only one or the other.

Give me Scotty any day. Scotty was real. He was joyful. He was
soulful. He was complete. He was the one to who everyone had to
turn in order to get the job done. Without Scotty, Kirk was merely a
raging bull on the bridge—shouting orders, fuming, and fussing.
Spock could use logic until the Tribbles came home, but Scotty

made Kirk's vision and Spock's mission flesh. He got the ship where it needed to go.

Of course, when all else failed he beamed them there. A friend of mine has been working on a concept of education, which she calls Transport-all© It is the notion that school is a gateway—both a portal and a journey where children must be taken from one place to another. If public education is to succeed in the future, all of them will have to make the journey.

SCHOOLS AS TRANSPORTERS

Scotty's machine for transporting the *Enterprise* crew was both a portal and a way of making the journey. It de-materialized the travelers and re-materialized them somewhere else. It took all of them— everyone who needed to go and all parts of the travelers themselves. Imagine what havoc would have ensued if Scotty had only beamed up their heads or their feet or if he had decided to rearrange their cells and molecules. What a mess.

Yet if we are honest with ourselves, we must admit that schools often deny the integrity of our children and try to make them into something else. We do this through failing to honor their cultures, their languages, their homes, or their learning styles. Yes, education is about transporting people to places they have never been before, but we also must see that they arrive intact, with their checked baggage also coming through with them.

As we look at the next millennium, it might be a good time for us to see our schools as portals to possibility and our roles as transporters of all our children. Beam us up, Scotty.

SECTION III

TRANSFORMING PUBLIC EDUCATION: CHALLENGES AND SOLUTIONS

20

LESSONS FROM ROOM 411

I think it was John Lennon who said life is what happens while you are busy making other plans. We all have had those moments when our reality confronts our intentions. Reality always wins.

About a year ago I was looking to the next day and all I had to do. Big plans, busy, busy. But that night I had a major tummy ache. Earlier episodes had been diagnosed as "acid reflux." But the pain would double me over and didn't seem to bear any relationship to the acid reflux others had described to me. Besides that, the medication I had been given didn't seem to help and the attacks were becoming more frequent and severe.

On my way to work I decided to stop by the doctor's office and see what could be done. I had gotten no sleep the night before and the pain had been quite memorable. A medical assistant saw me since my problems didn't seem to warrant a real doctor. Thank goodness for youth. In about 15 seconds he found I had a fever and abdominal pain and pointed out that is never a good combination. About 15 seconds more and he concluded my problem wasn't acid reflux but a gall bladder issue. The next thing I knew I was driving myself to the emergency room, instead of my office, and the following day I had major surgery to remove an infected gall bladder that had the biggest stone the surgeon had ever seen. Life is what happens while you are busy making other plans.

MULLING SYSTEMS

That started a week-long odyssey through the medical system that I found as enlightening as it was frustrating. Several of the lessons reinforced my commitment to systems thinking.

As my digestive system shut down, it created pressure on the diaphragm and I couldn't breathe properly. This led to a case of pneumonia. The shortage of oxygen created a shortage of enriched blood to my system. I had a severe potassium shortage, which it turns out endangers the heart. So I just lay in that hospital bed and watched one system within me pull another system down, which pulled another down.

Those of you who know me will not be surprised to know that naturally my thoughts turned to song. It was the one about how one bone is connected to another bone and so on. All my bones and systems were interconnected and when one started to fail it caused others to fail.

Fortunately, the medical staff wasn't about to let that happen so I had more tubes in me than a sixties television set and over time they got the digestive system back up, which took the pressure off the respiratory system allowing me to fight off the pneumonia, which got more oxygen to my system and the systems started to pull each other up.

Systems thinking is really an understanding that things are connected in an organic way. Sadly, our current reform efforts ignore this reality. And sadly, many good school leaders fail in their mission because they are trying to fix the pieces instead of healing the whole.

HIERARCHICAL TALK

But back to Arlington Hospital. As I observed the staff, I discovered on the one hand they had a system for everything. If you had a test scheduled for a certain time, they worked your medicine and nourishment around that (the tray of inedible food showed up in time to allow you not to eat it before going off for the test). The transport folks showed up when they were supposed to and the test clinicians were in their place ready to do their thing. I think we could learn a lot in systems work by observing the medical profession and how it handles these issues. Great planning at every turn.

However, I saw something that made me worry, not just about patients but about our students. Because, with all their systems, they still didn't communicate with each other. There seemed to be a strict hierarchy at work. Surgeons lived on their own planet. Like the rock stars they thought they were, they barely were seen outside of the surgery rooms and then didn't really deign to speak to mere mortals. The general practitioners interacted with the patient and the residents. The residents talked to the interns. No one talked to the nurses who were really the only people who knew what was happening with the patient.

The practical outcome was that you need an advocate watching things at all times or you will be given the wrong medication or have the wrong procedure done. As I watched all this happening, I wondered how much of this goes on in our schools. We know policy makers aren't really listening to professional educators. But what happens within our own circle? Do superintendents care what principals think? Do principals honor the opinions of their teachers? Does anyone ask the children how they are feeling or what they want? Is anyone listening to anyone else? What happens to good education when the listening system breaks down? And do the children who really need an advocate have one?

REALITY RULES

Now, my little story has a happy ending. I survived, minus one nasty gall bladder. In a few weeks I felt better than ever. I got back to making plans. So while you are out there making your plans, try to remember they need to have a systems approach to them if you have any expectation for success.

And try to listen a little more. And see that your children have a protector. And understand most of it is out of your control. One of my favorite jokes is the one that asks, "Do you know how to make God laugh? Tell Him you have a plan." You can plan for the future. Just don't expect reality to cooperate with you.

21

BURNING THOUGHTS ON A SNOWY DAY

L ast winter I was sitting in my office feeling kind of cozy. While the cold bitter wind whipped flurries outside my window, I looked around my comfortable office at my art on the walls, my books lining the shelves, and at plaques, diplomas, and mementos I had earned. I was looking around because I was "thinking"—at least that is what I claim it is if someone catches me looking around instead of working.

As I continued to "think," I looked out the window across the street where a massive building is being constructed. I have closely followed the progress of the demolition of the old building, the clearing of the debris, and the steady rise of the new building. It has given me many hours of thinking pleasure.

On this day I noticed the dozens of workers crawling around the open steel beams and concrete floors, struggling with the discomforts and dangers of a blustery, snowy winter day. They didn't have the advantages of my nice office. They didn't even have a safety net to catch them if they fell. Most of these workers are immigrants from Central and South America. Their office is open, dangerous, and uncomfortable. They work in the cold and live with the danger. How is it that I am lucky enough to be safe and warm here, and they are over there working much harder, under horrible conditions for less money?

THE RIGHT PLACE

One explanation is what rags-to-riches investor, philanthropist and writer Chris Gardner calls "place-ism." Gardner, author of the best-selling biography *The Pursuit of Happyness* upon which the Academy Award–nominated film is based, told the audience of the AASA National Conference in March 2007 that he ended up home-less on the streets because of being in the wrong place at the wrong time—hence, place-ism. It is something that can happen to anyone. I am in this warm office because of it. I was born on the right side of the border in every respect.

I was given the gift of education. I had teachers who saw more in me than I saw in myself and who would accept nothing less than my best. They believed in me and would not allow me to doubt myself. While I didn't have the advantages of the best schools, in our culture even less than the best is more than enough.

Education is such a personal interaction between the learner and the opportunity that the possibility of learning can be all that is needed if the student is willing. The difference in our culture between those with all the advantages and those with fewer is that the margin of error is greater for the "haves" than the "have-nots." They can afford more mistakes and to overlook possibilities. Those with less have to grab the brass ring when it appears because there may not be a second chance. So I sit in this office because I took advantage of what has been offered to me.

But I also sit here because I was not only in the right place but of the "right" race. I didn't have to overcome the stigma of skin color. Sadly, race still plays a major role in our society. If you don't think so, look out my window at the brown faces working in the danger and the bitter cold while most of the people in the warm comfortable offices have a lighter skin tone. We have made great progress on this front in overcoming our history, but the task is far from finished.

Racism is an interesting pathology, for it is based on the judg-ments one person makes of another built from external and superfi-cial observations. In making the judgment, the one being judged is being thought of as somehow less than the one judging.

Racism is an incredibly impersonal phenomenon because it makes no attempt to look past the outside to examine what is inside the heart and soul of another. It is also destructive because it mini-mizes and marginalizes the victim. Historically, it has been used as a means of controlling and keeping others down.

A New Pathology

All this led me to think about a new pathology facing our children. It too is a judgment made out of superficial and simplistic assessments of who they are and what they know, and these assessments can cause them to be seen as "less than." Let's call this pathology "testism."

Testism uses the blunt instrument of a multiple-choice questionnaire to determine what a person knows and doesn't know. It is used to determine their place and in doing so to determine their future. When we use an instrument that is overly simplistic and merely external to judge another person, we are not being fair. If we go further to use that instrument to keep a person in a lesser place, we are being destructive and inhuman. And if that person is also the victim of place-ism or racism as is the case with so many of our children, then the judgment is devastating.

The concept of high-stakes tests that will determine a child's future in terms of promotion and graduation is simply one more example of a superficial and external judgment being made that lessens the other person. The goal of education should be to liberate children from the places they have been assigned by life and to allow them to pursue their dreams. Tests will not do that. Norm-referenced tests that depersonalize the educational process can lead our next generation to the same victimization that we have worked so hard to move away from in past generations.

Will we have another generation that must face the cold and the danger of working in jobs that are less than our own because we have made judgments about them based upon superficial and limited information? Is this what we want for our own children? It's something to think about.

22

THE SEVEN DEADLY SINS OF NO CHILD LEFT BEHIND

H ave you ever considered that the remedy for being lost is not to drive faster? You have to stop and change direction. For five years the major school reform agenda in America has been the No Child Left Behind (NCLB) Act, which was part of the most recent reauthorization of the Elementary and Secondary Education Act (ESEA). Now ESEA is up for another reauthorization by Congress, and everyone is wondering what is going to happen next. It has been suggested that NCLB be expanded to high schools or that more interventions or national standards be required. But more is not the solution. It is time to change direction.

It is now universally accepted, even by those who authored the bill, that NCLB is flawed and needs fixing. In fact, describing the law as flawed might be charitable. If you take the definition of "sin" as a "shameful offense," then it could be argued that NCLB is full of sin because it has proved itself to be an offense against good education. For that reason, merely adding a growth model to the accountability provisions or creating some additional flexibility for English-language learners will not fix the underlying structural weaknesses of the law. Neither will adding more money. You can't get something designed for one purpose to be effective at fulfilling a very different purpose, no matter how many resources you apply to it. While there are aspects of the law that could be fixed, there are flaws in it that are so fundamental that there is not enough paint and spackle in the world to make them presentable.

Many will dismiss any criticism of NCLB now just as they have dismissed previous criticism. In the past, critics have been accused of exhibiting "the soft bigotry of low expectations" and have been labeled "apologists for a failed system." The generic response to critics has been that educators don't want to be held accountable. Now the contention is that America is failing to remain competitive in the global economy and that if we don't put more rigor into the education system our children will not be able to compete. None of these retorts are accurate or particularly useful.

THE NEED FOR A SYSTEMIC SOLUTION

One could argue that there is much in the U.S. education system that is not effective and needs to change and that NCLB's focus on accountability has helped to illuminate this need. Some educators may have held inappropriately low expectations for their students, so requiring schools to disaggregate test-score data by race, disability, socioeconomic status, and English proficiency helps make certain that schools do not paper over the lack of success of some of their students. But the most fundamental problem facing education is that the current system is perfectly designed to yield the current results. If we are not happy with the current results, a systemic solution is called for. NCLB, which adopts assessment as its key strategy, does not begin to deal with education in a systemic way.

The deadly sins of NCLB are largely the result of a set of wrong assumptions about the problems facing schools and children. If we continue to fix things that are not really broken, we will simply break those things that work while the real problems go unattended.

Sin No. 1: Assuming that schools are broken.

Most education reform is driven by a belief that the system is badly broken and must be fixed. In fact, the system is quite successful in fulfilling its historical mission of preparing children for an agricultural and industrial economy. It is not broken. It is a well-oiled machine doing the wrong thing.

The problem is that the world now requires a different set of skills. Indeed, the jobs that the education system was designed to fill are in short supply. What is required is a hard look at what schools need to produce and then a total retooling aimed at achieving that end. Schools haven't failed at their mission. The mission has changed.

Some might argue that NCLB will lead to the retooling needed in education. But that is true only if you believe that the road to the future is paved with low-level tests that measure discrete bits of knowledge. The reality is that anyone in business will tell you that successful workers in the new global economy must have skills of collaboration, ingenuity, problem solving, comfort with ambiguity, and a dozen other things—none of which are tested for and subsequently taught as a result of NCLB. Schools that focus on twenty-first-century skills are doing so in spite of NCLB, not because of it.

The truth is that many schools and school systems in the United States work remarkably well for most students. Furthermore, the system is made up of over 50 million children, over 95,000 schools, and over 14,000 districts. Most of these children, schools, and districts are pretty successful, even under the restrictive expectations of NCLB. Even using AYP (adequate yearly progress) under NCLB as a measure, most kids meet most of the standards. Were it not for the "all or nothing" aspect of the scoring system, only a small fraction of the schools in America would be having difficulty making AYP.

And even the harshest critic of public education must admit that the majority of students are not failing. Nevertheless, we have constructed a federally mandated system that treats all school districts, schools, and children pretty much the same—whether they are failing or succeeding dramatically. Would a business that has a high failure rate in one factory and a low one in another subject both to the same treatment? Would a doctor treat a patient with a head cold the same way she would treat one with lung cancer? Any rational response to our educational challenges would examine the range of school performance and act accordingly.

Sin No. 2: Conflating testing with education.

Testing is an important part of the educational process. Teachers need to know what kids know and how they are progressing, and the public has a right to have a snapshot of how well benchmarks are being met. But testing must be kept in perspective. A number of states were making significant progress on their statewide plans before NCLB was implemented, and they had to step back from more sophisticated uses of assessments to meet the lower standards set by NCLB.

When student achievement is discussed, it has now come to mean test results. Yet the least sophisticated citizen among us understands that there is much more to education than what can be tested. When our sole emphasis is squarely on a single aspect of education, the entire process gets distorted. One of the greatest dangers posed by NCLB is that we will reach a point where most kids meet an acceptable standard set by the tests but do so at the expense of a broader and deeper learning experience. Setting standards can be useful, but only if the standards do not lead to standardization. A wise man once pointed out to me that training makes people alike and education makes them different. If we put too much emphasis on a lower, common denominator, we will be sacrificing higher possibilities for our children.

Sin No. 3: Harming poor children and ignoring the realities of poverty.

ESEA was originally created to address the needs of poor and minority children. While great strides have been made, much remains to be done.

Those who wrote and voted for NCLB ostensibly did so out of a belief that we should not leave some children behind. However, broadening the law's requirements well beyond those most in need to include all schools and all children has caused educators to take their eyes off the ball. A recent study showed that the children closest to making AYP, not those most in need of assistance, are the ones receiving the bulk of the attention. Drilling poor students on basic skills while their middle-class counterparts partake of a richer curriculum will not close the real learning gap between students. It simply further limits the possibilities for poor children.

While Washington has created a system that ostensibly helps poor children, it doesn't want to talk about the impact of poverty on school success. Those who see poverty as an intervening variable have been accused of having lowered expectations for disadvantaged children. This has meant there has been no real discussion about what might be needed to *really* leave no child behind. While history is replete with stories of heroic exceptions (e.g., Lincoln was born in a log cabin and became president), there is no evidence that whole groups of people have been elevated by ignoring the chains that bind them.

Everyone in America knew which children were being left behind long before NCLB became law. A massive system of testing was not required. When you are born without adequate prenatal care, when you do not have sufficient health care as a toddler, when your parents do not know how to provide cognitive stimulation and cannot afford high-quality preschool programs, chances are you will come to school with a working vocabulary that is just a fraction of the vocabularies of middle-class children. You have already been left behind.

Still, most educators put their shoulders to the wheel and try to push it uphill anyway. Sometimes they succeed. But when they fail, as they often do, they know that any law that fails to acknowledge the broader systemic issues that cause some children to be hobbled by circumstances is a law that will not work. The sad fact is that schools can and should help disadvantaged children—but schools can't do it all. Leaving no child behind also requires us to leave no family and no community behind.

The inequities that exist between school districts and between states further complicate the issue. For example, the children in Cuyahoga Heights, Ohio, receive twice as much financial support for their schools as do the children in nearby East Cleveland. Yet the taxpayers in Cuyahoga Heights have to tax themselves only about one-third as much as those in East Cleveland in order to create this unequal result. At the same time, children in California are not getting nearly the same level of school support that the children of Connecticut get.

How can we pretend to have a national law that holds educators accountable for outcomes when the resources are so uneven? Put most simply, some children get left behind because our society, through a series of policy decisions, has chosen to leave them behind. Testing and sanctions on schools will not change that reality.

Sin No. 4: Relying on fear and coercion.

Motivation has always been the key to good education. Unfortunately, NCLB relies for motivation on the blunt force of threats and punishments. It starts by assuming that those at the top know better than those farther down the line, even though those nearest the bottom are charged with actually doing what is needed to educate children. By using fear and coercion as a change strategy, NCLB ensures compliance but blocks the pursuit of excellence for teachers and children. While you can beat people into submission, you can't beat them into greatness.

You can't inspire children by means that either turn them off or traumatize them. Children are subjected to days of examinations annually, with the time taken away from instruction. Indeed, we have actually reduced the time we spend on instruction so that we can increase the time we spend on measuring the results of instruction. To offset this, many schools have chosen to neglect subjects not covered by the tests, so that the curriculum has narrowed. Many children have chosen to turn off and not try. Others have felt traumatized by the pressure. Cognitive scientists are clear that the emotion of fear blocks clear thinking by impeding neural processing. Any educational model that relies on fear undercuts its own aims.

Collaboration, not coercion, is what is needed. While most educators believe accountability is an important part of the public education experience, supporters of NCLB fail to see that other options for accountability exist. Accountability systems will work only where there is collaboration and trust between the federal government and the schools. Good accountability systems would be broader in nature and would actually allow us to examine the broader needs of a child's learning.

Sin No. 5: Lacking clarity.

Any accountability system should be clear and understandable to those it is accountable to: parents and other citizens. Most parents find the AYP model to be confusing and, when explanations are given, counterintuitive. Why would you measure completely different groups in the same way and compare the results? Why would a school that fails to make progress in one cell be treated the same as one that fails to make progress in all cells? Why would you hold special education children, who have individual education plans because of their needs, to the same standard as children who do not have the same needs? Why would you test children in English when they do not yet speak English? Any accountability system needs to have a sense of authenticity if it is to be useful.

Sin No. 6: Leaving out the experts.

Those at the federal level do not—and cannot—know better how to educate a child than those working at the child's level. In other professions, while guidelines are created for public safety, bureaucrats don't try to second-guess the work of professionals who deliver services. For example, pilots, while subject to rules and regulations, are still presumed to know better how to fly the plane than their passengers. No federal law that takes the professionals out of the decision-making process will ever work. Professional judgment must be taken into account if we have any hope that NCLB will work. Jamming a comprehensive set of mandates down the throats of those who must carry out the mandates is doomed—not just because of the insurgency it creates, but because many ideas that look so good in Washington just don't work in Weehawken.

Sin No. 7: Undermining our international competitiveness.

Finally, the greatest sin committed by NCLB is a sin of omission. NCLB fails to address the core question for America: How do we sustain our place in a global environment? NCLB's answer is that drilling our children will allow them to compete with the Chinese. Yet the real winners in the coming competition between East and West will not be the nations that focus on basic skills but those that cultivate high-level skills and ingenuity. In that regard, America has had an edge for some time.

Our society seems to produce unusually creative and entrepreneurial people. Most of those people went to our public schools. In fact, much of America's creativity emanated from those in our society who had been left behind. Whether in music, sports, or technology, innovation comes from the edge, where many of those children who are left behind congregate. These individuals have enormous capacity to lift our society to new levels through their creativity.

Harvard psychologist Ellen Langer has pointed out that fear of evaluation, an acceptance of absolutes, and mindless ideas about our mistakes can stop us from being creative and responsive to the world. She has said that such mental paralysis comes from "anything hierarchical [that] suggests that there is a single metric—a 'right' way of understanding the world." If America is to continue to lead the world, we must begin to undo the damage created by a system that is built upon the notion that there is a single right way to do education.

How can we sustain our creativity while paring down our education to a stimulus-response system of learning that reduces knowledge to a series of test bubbles and communicates to children that what is on the test is the only thing worth learning? The great danger we face is that, in our rush to build skills, we undermine our wisdom. Then we will all be left behind. For that reason NCLB needs to be deposited in the dustbin of history, and Congress, with the assistance of educators and other citizens, needs to think more broadly and deeply about how to build on and make use of the talents of our poorest citizens.

A NEW AGENDA FOR EDUCATION

It's easy enough to level criticisms when a law such as NCLB misses its mark by so wide a margin. But what would a new agenda for U.S. education look like? The following steps can serve as an initial blueprint for building a new agenda for U.S. education.

1. Fix the assumptions. Stop the blame game. Put an emphasis on systemic thinking that looks at what it would take to retool the education system to respond to the new mission of preparing all children to reach their highest levels. Stop blaming the professional educators who must carry out this retooling, and construct a system that supports their work. Create schools that children want to go to, schools that emphasize meaningful and engaged learning and acknowledge that imagination is as vital at age 18 as at age 5.

2. Put testing in context and emphasize depth in education. Put the emphasis on testing into a broader context. Use models to measure

growth, but continue to find ways of disaggregating data to allow schools to see clearly where they are succeeding and where improvements are needed. Challenge schools to continue to emphasize the depth and breadth of education. Help schools shift from a "coverage" mentality to one that focuses on depth and "metacognition." Emphasize that the work of schools is educating children, not training them. Put the focus on educating the whole child, not just the parts that decode and cipher.

3. Use a change strategy that emphasizes collaboration. Take a page from the Irish playbook and create a new model of accountability that creates a collaboration between states and local districts in which the role of states is to build capacity for change and improvement at the local level. Create a system of ensuring quality that touches on all the major parts of the learning process. Restore a sense of trust and mutual support.

4. Focus on a strategy for addressing poor children. Go back to the intent of ESEA and focus the money and effort on those who most need help. Forget about trying to use a limited program to "reform" all of American education. Understand that just as nation building in other countries requires enormous resources, so does dealing with the plight of poor children at home. End what I call the "hard bigotry of inadequate resources" by developing a Marshall Plan for America's Poor that provides adequate health care and preschool programs for those in need and creates "human enterprise zones" where large numbers of poor children live. Stop pretending that money doesn't matter. The only people who believe that are people with money.

5. Renew America's commitment to innovation. Require and support the teaching of art, music, and drama in all of America's schools. Make certain that any language assessment includes creative writing. Develop programs that value and support innovative thinking in schools. Put a new emphasis on a broad program of gifted education. Require any new mandate in education to undergo an "innovation protection assessment" to make certain that it does not unintentionally undermine creativity. Emphasize attracting and keeping creative teachers and leaders in our schools by enacting a new version of the National Defense Education Act

that supports students going into teaching and forgives the student loans of those who teach in hard-to-staff schools. Create a dialogue—a real two-way conversation—between America's educators and business leaders about what we need to do to maintain America's innovative edge.

This article first appeared in the June 2007 issue of the Phi Delta Kappan Magazine.

23

AUTHENTIC ACCOUNTABILITY

Is there anyone at this point who believes that public schools should *not* be accountable? The notion of accountability is so widespread it should be added to the list of apple pie and motherhood as those things most genuinely American.

The issue is no longer whether accountability is good or bad or here to stay. The interesting thing is that school leaders want to be held accountable because it is the only way the issue of value can be validated. If you work hard to improve student learning, you need some way of demonstrating it is happening and you are succeeding.

Further, accountability provides a tool of leverage for leaders to move their systems so many embrace it simply for that reason alone. It is also clear politicians like the notion of accountability and will see to it that it is built into future legislation. So for the record, let's stipulate that accountability is a given in the educational environment.

A BROADER VIEW

Accountability is appropriate in a public entity that serves and is funded by the public. However, there are serious problems with the current accountability structure. It assumes that accountability and student achievement are the same thing; yet when you survey the public, as AASA has, you find they have a much broader view of what accountability means. The public looks for accountability in the way money is used and accounted for. It looks for a more transparent and accessible accountability system, one that is clear on what it is doing and how it is doing it and one that gives the public access to the system. Student achievement information is but one piece of the information the public wants.

So the first lesson for school leaders is that they must take a much broader view of accountability from what they are currently being required to do.

Further, we have conflated student achievement and test scores. These two things are treated as synonymous when, in fact, they are quite different. Student test scores are at best a proxy for a relatively small portion of the learning that should take place in school. They reflect a narrow band of understanding as demonstrated with multiple-choice responses by the student. They do not demonstrate deep thinking or the critical elements of being a full human being such as creativity, courage or compassion.

A real measure of student achievement should reflect a much broader aspect of student learning than what can be garnered from a standardized test, which will only yield a rough comparison of a student's limited understanding of a band of information with how students of a similar age answer the same questions. As Albert Einstein was reported to have said, not everything that is counted counts and not everything that counts can be counted.

Most importantly we need to examine to whom the schools are being held accountable. Current models were constructed by high-level federal officials and members of Congress. State systems were created by state bureaucracies and statewide elected officials. The models and reporting systems were sculpted to yield scores that could fit bureaucratic scoring sheets. They were not explained to the public. Perhaps that is because when they are explained they make little sense. The NCLB model that compares the scores of one group with scores of another group and then purports to measure "progress" makes little sense to educators and even less to parents.

The concept of adequate yearly progress sounds good, but the various categories of reporting make little rational sense. Children who cannot speak enough English to understand the test are tested in English anyway and expected to make progress. Children who have individual education plans because of a learning disability have to be measured against other children without those same conditions.

IDEA has been in place for more than 30 years and is based on the correct notion that children with learning disabilities must be addressed with those disabilities in mind. NCLB says it does not matter. The bottom line is that accountability is only a concept that works if people understand it and agree with its fairness.

PUBLIC DESIRES

The reality is that the public schools belong to the public. It pays for them. As democracy scholar Benjamin Barber once pointed out, public schools not only serve the public, they create the public. Accountability will only become meaningful when it becomes authentic to the stakeholders who matter most—the parents and the public. Accountability systems must reflect the needs and expectations of those the system is serving. Authentic accountability should start by finding out what the public wants to know and how that knowledge can be packaged to be meaningful to parents and the next-door neighbors.

We know that people see education in a broad way. They want to see kids do well on basic skills, but they also need to do well in areas that are basic to living—being good citizens, productive members of the community and able to find and hold down a job that allows them to live in America.

And we know, strange as it might sound to bureaucrats and "coercocrats" who want to control the system from their exalted perches, that parents, above all else, want to see their children happy. While those who impose accountability systems on others have a hard time relating to happiness as a goal, our forefathers got it. The "pursuit of happiness" was a basic tenet of our founding fathers. That should be the foundation of authentic accountability.

24

BARKING UP THE
RIGHT TREE

*What if our society's future economic health belongs to the artists,
storytellers, and poets—and not the scientists and engineers?*

There is a childhood saying about a confused dog who thinks he
sees a possum in a tree. The problem is that the possum is
actually in a different tree so the dog barks up the wrong tree.
American education is constantly playing both dog and possum.
Sometimes we are the prey, and sometimes we are just confused
about what and where the prey is.

The last few years have revealed growing concern about U.S.
global competitiveness, particularly against a backdrop of the rising
economic power of India and China. This is not unlike concern in the
1980s with Japan and Germany. But this time the competition looms
larger, and the stakes are higher. This topic has been regularly addressed
in the news, and corporate CEOs and governors have weighed in with
their views, as has President Bush in his 2006 State of the Union
address. The hysteria could best be summed up in a paraphrase of a
40-year-old saying, as "the Asians are coming, the Asians are coming."

Undoubtedly, the ascendance of China as an economic power
and of India as a place where many American jobs go to die has
raised legitimate concerns. Thomas Friedman, author of the best-
selling book *The World Is Flat,* suggests that with the rise of China
and India, America will have to run faster just to say in place.

Today, hardly an American CEO can be found who does not look with awe and concern at what is happening on the other side of the world. Many U.S. businesses have shipped work and jobs to both India and China, and, as with every previous threat to American dominance, our schools have been called to account for failing to produce enough engineers and math and science workers to compete with this rising threat.

The education solutions offered are that we should make our students work harder and study more math and science. And we need more and harder tests to motivate them to do so.

A SOPHISTICATED ANSWER

The problem with this thinking is that it just isn't that simple. First, the math doesn't add up for the United States. Both India and China are massive countries. If they educate only their elites, they will still have a huge edge in available knowledge workers. America could make all its children high-tech workers, and we would still be out-numbered. Further, an engineer in either Beijing or Bangalore will work for a fraction of the wages of her American counterpart. To remain competitive, our workers would have to take monumental pay cuts, with attendant reductions in lifestyle, simply to hold their own. If we were to stop at this point, despair would seem the only rational response.

The good news is that there is more to the story—a right tree to bark up, so to speak. Put most simply, America should compete at what it has always done best: being the innovative engine that drives the world economy. To do that will require increased efforts at pro-ducing more highly talented engineers and technical workers. But we must improve the way we teach math and science by making these subjects more engaging to more students.

Yet there is also a bigger issue emerging. Daniel Pink in his provocative book, *A Whole New Mind,* has gone so far as to declare that the Information Age is nearing an end and that we are entering the "conceptual age." He argues that the dominance of the "left-brain-driven" world, where everything is sequential and logical, is giving way to a more "right-brained" endeavor that focuses on the creative, holistic skills.

Pink suggests that if you have a job that can be done by a machine, can be done cheaper, or can be done somewhere else, you have cause to worry. Those who work on conceptual and creative work—design, storytelling, and the like—will dominate in this new world. He turns the current discussion upside down. It isn't about how many engineers a nation has. Rather it's about how many artists and poets it produces. These are the individuals who can create the new meaning necessary in a conceptual world.

Richard Florida, in his book *Rise of the Creative Class,* makes similar arguments. The future belongs to the creative. They will be the leaders, the earners and the learners of the new age. It is not the programmers in India who will dominate; it is the people who conceive of the work the programmers should do who will "rule."

Already we know that most of the places where America has an economic edge are where our creative workers have gone before. For example, our popular culture, best exemplified by the entertainment industry, is a major export for the United States, and in fact it might be argued that "the American Century," as some called the twentieth century, came about not simply because of our economic or military might but because we were the source of the images and sounds people savored. Even our high-tech industries have found their dominance at the edge of such work, creating new concepts of the way work should be done or "imagineering" (as the Disney folks call it) new ways of doing things.

While it is important that our children be educated to be comfortable with and conversant in the languages of math and science, and while we need to continue to produce our fair share of technical workers, the future will not be created by these folks. The future will be created by those who can dream bigger and more innovative dreams.

SCHOOLING'S IMPACT

The implications for education are profound. We must reexamine how we teach children and what we teach them. I was one of those students who grew up hating math and science. I wasn't much happier with social studies and language arts. As an adult educator I finally came to understand why. When I became superintendent of schools in Princeton, New Jersey, I was thrown into an environment rife with Nobel laureates and world-class theoretical mathematicians and physicists. And I made a profound discovery in talking with them. I found out that the math I learned in school had the same relationship to mathematics as a log has to a blueberry.

Mathematics wasn't about mastering rules; it was about discovering the elegance of a well-stated problem. Further, science is not about mastering the periodic table and a series of formulas, it is about seeking answers to the mysteries of the universe. Likewise, social studies isn't about dates and events, it is about understanding the human condition, and literature is a way of coming to understand more about ourselves.

If we expect our children to become more adept in all of these subjects, we must begin to educate our teachers to be more knowledgeable about their subject matter and to be more creative in the way material is presented. Teachers must be designers and storytellers. Further, school leaders must reassess their roles as instructional leaders. How do we reinvent the learning process so that it becomes meaningful and engaging for students, so they are motivated by more than a test or benchmark? As one student, quoted in a recent *Time* magazine cover story on the current science crisis, said, "I associated engineering with long, boring assignments. No one showed me why it was cool."

We have to find a way to make learning relevant and "cool." We can do that only by having teachers who are supported in using their own creativity. So how do we recruit and support teachers who see themselves as artists? Sadly, with the way we currently approach schooling in America, we are destined to become a third-rate economy and a third-world power. We are forfeiting our greatest edge by walking away from what we do best.

In a *Newsweek* commentary last January, Fareed Zakaria described a conversation about education that he had with people in Asia. China has increased its spending on colleges and universities tenfold in the past decade. This comes at a time when states in the United States, which cut taxes during the boom years of the 1990s, are struggling to hold their own in education spending and when the recent federal budget proposed to cut support for education by more than $12 billion. Clearly it will be hard to maintain our edge without investment.

Zakaria's commentary also pointed out that America has slowed its investment in research and development at the very time other countries have accelerated theirs. The United States currently ranks seventh in percentage of gross domestic product devoted to research spending.

UNTESTED QUALITIES

But money isn't the only issue. Zakaria talked with the minister of education in Singapore, a city-state that is often compared to the United States in education. Singapore is the top-ranked nation in the global rankings of children's performance in science and math. Zakaria asked the minister to explain why it is that, even though the Singaporean students do so well on these tests, when you look at the same students 10 to 20 years later, few are world beaters. American students, by contrast, test much worse but seem to do better in life and the real world—particularly as inventors and entrepreneurs.

The minister explained that both countries have meritocracies. America's is based on talent; Singapore's is based on test scores. Because we cannot effectively test much of the intellect, such as creativity, curiosity, ambition, or a sense of adventure, the tests don't measure areas where America has an edge.

The minister further explained that America's culture of learning challenges conventional wisdom, even to the point of challenging authority. He suggested that these are areas in which Singapore must learn from America. He ended by explaining that the problem in America is that poor children are not brought along and that very bright children are allowed to coast.

TEST PREOCCUPATION

America is currently caught up in a frenzy of test-based reform, designed ostensibly to benefit those most likely to be left behind. The problem is that this authoritarian model, which emphasizes the achievement of the left brain, is doomed to fail with many of these children. And the failure will not be because students do not test well; there is every indication that when emphasis is put on tests, the scores rise. Just ask Singapore.

The real test will be faced when we ask whether this increase in scores will lead to increased life success for these students. And this brings us back to the premise of Pink's work—that the future belongs to the creative. The "test and tremble" model of school reform that is the current craze, which values a score over broader success, is unlikely to move us toward a more conceptual and creative society.

In fact, with the emphasis placed so solidly on basic reading and math, the creative activities that Pink espouses (art, music, and creative expression generally) are being squeezed out of the curriculum.

Ellen Langer, in her book *Mindfulness,* suggests that an education that is based on an outcomes model leads in fact to "mindlessness." She points out that from kindergarten on, schooling usually focuses on goals rather than on the processes needed to achieve them. She says, "When children start a new activity with an outcome orientation, questions of 'can I' or 'what if I can't' are likely to predominate, creating an anxious preoccupation with success or failure rather than drawing on the child's natural, exuberant desire to explore."

We know from brain researchers that fear inhibits cognitive ability. An educational model based on coercive strategies is doomed to undo the very thing it is trying to create—a smarter and more capable America.

The major goal of American education under No Child Left Behind is to "close the achievement gap," which as the minister of education from Singapore noted exists because America has a large underclass that has not been educated to the highest possible levels. This problem is pretty universally accepted. The question is whether an educational model that focuses on outcomes and deficits will close the gap or whether a different approach—one that focuses on a broader definition of education and focuses on assets—will work better.

LAUDABLE CAPACITIES

The irony of our current educational angst over poor and minority children is that the same children who cannot read well can create and remember incredibly complex song lyrics set to hip-hop music. In fact, much of America's creativity in music came from blues, jazz, rock 'n' roll, and rap, all products of the so-called underclass.

Further, children who cannot spell "systems thinking" demonstrate an understanding of the movement of 10 people on a basketball court as they move through time and space at high speeds and are able to anticipate future moves and instantly create elegant responses to them. Children who have trouble following a teacher's instructions can shift language and culture numerous times a day, and children who have trouble with basic math can create intricate designs and artistic creations.

The good news is that much of America's creative expression has come from the very people we worry about not having received a great "left brain" education. But as creativity and invention grow in importance, the assets that are already present simply need to be nurtured. Is there a way for America to rediscover its competitive edge, not by becoming more like the Asians, but by being more like Americans? Is there a way to use the inherent talents that many of our underperforming children exhibit in nonschool activities and bring those talents into the classroom by helping teachers focus on the assets the children have and by honoring their thinking skills and ways of looking at the world?

Isn't it time we started barking up the right tree?

This essay first appeared in the September 2006 issue of the Phi Delta Kappan Magazine.

25

INTELLIGENT REDESIGN

Reframing the Discussion on
High School Reform

W hen the most powerful man in the world and the richest man in the world agree on something, attention must be paid. President Bush has made high school reform a centerpiece of his second term, and Microsoft Corp. chairman Bill Gates has been putting his money where his mouth is by massively funding high school reform efforts. Both men, along with most of the nation's governors and business leaders, have concluded that our high schools are badly broken and that something must be done.

Before we get too carried away, however, let's consider several problems with the current discussion about high school reform. Anyone with a short-term memory will realize we have seen this movie before. It starts with an avalanche of crisis rhetoric, supported by selective data. Then it is decided that the solution involves making people work harder; pressure is put on the system by adding more tests, and then the powers that be move on to the next big reform. It happened after Sputnik, it happened after *A Nation at Risk,* and it has been happening with the No Child Left Behind Act.

The real problem in discussing high school reform is that, quite simply, anything you want to say about high schools is true—and false. With over 18,600 high schools, you can find the good, the bad, and the ugly. America can claim that it has some of the best high schools in the world, and it does. But there are others that aren't so great, and some that few of us would want to be around. Some high schools are incredibly boring places where kids are allowed to put in their seat time in exchange for a diploma. But others are vibrant and exciting places. Perhaps we should learn from them before we reinvent the system—one more time.

We have been reforming high schools since they were created. So before we rush too far down the reform highway, perhaps we should find out why folks don't feel they are reformed yet. There are a number of reasons, but chief among them is that we haven't reached a consensus on what high schools are supposed to do. Western society has created a waiting room for young people called "adolescence," which is a purgatory between childhood and adulthood, and high schools are where we put them until they ripen. It can be argued that in some communities high schools have become holding pens for the disinterested. The schools' main task, in this mode, is to keep teenagers off the streets and out of adults' hair until they can move on. In other communities, high schools are prep schools for later life—a place to "get ready" for adulthood by taking college-prep courses, or to prepare for a job through vocational training. In still other communities, they are beacons of excitement that run on the recognition that teenagers are living their lives now and have legitimate gifts and interests that should be supported.

The first question is whether all our high schools need to be reformed. And the second, related question is, Do we need another federal intervention to make things better? Perhaps all we need is an "intelligent redesign" to identify the real problems and solve them.

The reality is that, like a lot of other aspects of American education, high schools are asked to be all things to all people. Yet, they are shaped by the communities in which they exist. Communities with resources tend to have more vibrancy in their programs and better achievement. It is still true that the prime variable on SAT outcomes is family income—the richer the family, the higher the score. In other communities, we put students in facilities that more closely resemble factories or prisons and add to the burden they've already been given. Despite this, many less-affluent communities have been working hard at improving their schools, even without sufficient support. But we cannot build a system on heroic exceptions.

One major issue is that high schools are part of a bigger system. They are affected by the preparation students receive prior to arriving at their doors. They are also shaped by the expectations of colleges and employers. If we want a different result from our high schools, we need to look much more broadly at the context in which they exist. Failure to do so will lead to a continuation of piecemeal solutions and growing frustration.

A further reality is that there have been fairly intensive efforts at reforming high schools for over 20 years. People have not been waiting for politicians to discover high schools and the next great reform opportunity. The National Association of Secondary School Principals published a comprehensive reform document called "Breaking Ranks" in the early 1990s that has been a blueprint for reform. Schools have expanded graduation requirements. Since the publication of the federal report *A Nation at Risk* in 1983, the average number of Carnegie units earned by public school graduates has gone from 21 to 26. Schools have introduced more rigor into the curriculum. The number of schools offering Advanced Placement courses, for example, has gone from a little over 5,000 to more than 14,000 in the same 22-year time frame, the number of AP candidates has grown from about 175,000 to nearly a million, and the number of AP exams taken has risen from slightly under 200,000 to nearly 1.6 million. More students are taking more and harder courses. Meanwhile, the use of high-stakes tests has become a stick to wave at indolent students and teachers. At last count, more than 20 states had introduced some form of high-stakes graduation test, with more on the horizon.

So what is being suggested by our august leaders as the new path to reform? How are we to fix this "broken" system? Tougher curricula and more testing. I am reminded of one definition of insanity: doing the same thing over and over expecting a different result.

Alarmingly, as we have increased the rigor and the assessment, students' interest in school seems to have diminished. One survey of high school seniors showed that the percentage who found schoolwork always meaningful declined from 40 percent in 1983 to 28 percent in 2000. And the percentage who felt that school learning would be quite helpful in later life dropped from 51 percent to 39 percent. So we seem to be moving in the wrong direction. If we stay on this path, we will see a day when students take many more and harder courses, and none of them will see this as meaningful or useful.

What do we want the schools to be about, and what should we do in them to produce a different result? It may be instructive to hear from Intel Corp. CEO Craig Barrett, who is a board member of Achieve Inc., the business- and governor-sponsored reform group that co-hosted this year's national summit on high schools.

In a recent op-ed piece in *USA Today,* Mr. Barrett says, "The harsh fact is that the United States' need for the highest quality of human capital in science, mathematics, and engineering is not being met." He is quoting the U.S. Commission on National Security for the 21st Century and espousing a common expectation for our schools: to produce human capital for the international marketplace.

The "one simple reason we're lagging behind" the rest of the world, Mr. Barrett suggests, is that "we've institutionalized low performance through low expectations." "High schools," he writes, "expect only a small number of students to take the advanced math and science young people need." He goes on the say that until we feel more pain, there will be little motivation to change.

The Intel chief merely is stating what so many others believe: The function of schools is to be instrumental to the greater economy, and the reason schools don't do better is that they don't expect enough of themselves or their students. The solution is achieved by creating a greater sense of pain though threats of "accountability."

At some point we need to have a discussion on whether schools are a farm team for corporate America or should serve a broader goal of molding educated citizens who can pursue their dreams. No one would argue that having marketable skills to make a living is not necessary to pursuing one's dreams. But it can be argued that job skills, though necessary, are not sufficient to living a successful life.

Another discussion should be around the "low expectations" charge. Certainly there are teachers and schools that do not expect enough of their students. But it is also true that virtually all the successful adults I know are successful because a teacher believed in them and helped them believe in themselves.

We also should have a national discussion on how best to motivate educators and learners. Is there any evidence, for example, that you can bludgeon people to greatness or beat them to excellence?

Pain may be useful to encourage people to change, but is it helpful in sustaining the change?

Most of all, I want to take exception with the core of what Mr. Barrett and others believe can and should happen to make schools better.

The op-ed piece looks back fondly to the post-Sputnik era, when the United States awoke to the competition represented by the Soviet Union's exploits in space and pushed for excellence in mathematics and science. The push resulted in a dramatic increase in enrollments in engineering and science. I was in school myself during that era, and I can't recall that we felt much of a difference between pre- and post-Sputnik education. Ironically, what happened during that time was not a sweeping reform that greatly expanded the numbers of children getting access to a first-rate education so they could become scientists and engineers. What happened was an increase in gifted-and-talented programs for some, and better college scholarships for those who were interested in engineering and science.

In that era, the government even gave a lot of support to those who wanted to go into teaching, something we see much less of today. If we want better students, shouldn't we start by helping our teachers?

I read Mr. Barrett's essay on a plane to Kansas, where I was to visit a high school program in the city of Olathe. The school district there has developed a series of programs in all its high schools called "21st-Century Schools." These programs are vocational, in that they are focused on the future working lives of students. But they also are very rigorous academically and produce great results. Most important, they are interesting, engaging, and meaningful to the students. These are hands-on programs that use the students' motivation to create as a vehicle for excellence.

As I walked through Olathe Northwest High School during that visit, I saw students and teachers engaged in hard work. I'm quite sure they saw their work as meaningful and useful. In one classroom, the students were constructing a "battlebot," which is a robot used in gaming to battle other robots. The last one running is declared the winner. These students were looking forward to taking their creation to a national competition later this year.

While this kind of work is fun—some might say frivolous— what is really happening in the class is much deeper. Students are learning about metallurgy, structures, engines, insulation, and a hundred other difficult concepts now made concrete and under-standable. The Olathe students were excited about what they were doing—and yes, they were knowledgeable. They talked about how hard the project was—and how enjoyable.

There were 10 or 12 students who stayed after the bell to talk with me, and I found that every one of them plans to go to college to study engineering. In Olathe, it seems, there is no shortage of engineering candidates. I asked them why they liked what they were doing, and the answer was simple. One student told me he got to use what he was learning in class. "Telling me that calculus is good for me isn't very meaningful," he said. "Now I see how I can use it."

Those who want to reform high schools should start in places like Olathe, where the district has figured out that the best way to get students to learn more is to give them work that engages their imaginations and creates meaning for them. We have to give schools adequate resources, of course, to provide the kind of state-of-the-art opportunities that allow students to get their hands on the learning. And the learning must look to the future, not the past.

Those who are interested in reform should focus on getting schools the resources they need to do the job, and then challenging them to make schools interesting and engaging places. Reform will not work by putting on more handcuffs. It will be accomplished by removing shackles so that people can fly.

Education has always been about the whole child, and unless we take that into consideration, the current effort to reform high schools will be just as successful as all the others that preceded it.

This essay first appeared in Education Week. *Published online: June 14, 2005. Published in print: June 15, 2005. Reprinted with permission of the author.*

26

EINSTEIN'S BRAIN

On April 16, 1955, Albert Einstein died of heart failure in Princeton, New Jersey. Given the heart he had, it is hard to imagine it failing, but sometimes the physical lets the metaphysical down.

What I have always found interesting was that when doctors performed an autopsy on Einstein, shortly thereafter they discovered his brain was missing. Apparently it was removed during the autopsy so it could be studied and was misplaced. I'll leave it to you to think about the irony of that.

As we know, Einstein is considered the great genius of the twentieth century, and some scientist thought that by examining his brain we might learn the secret to his intelligence. Now I am confident we are all grateful that Einstein died before they removed his brain for study. If he were living in our current era, with our obsession for data, someone might have come up with the bright idea of removing his brain so we could weigh it, even if he were still using it.

In education, it's a long-standing joke that we pull up the trees to see if the roots are growing, so measuring someone's brain doesn't seem like a far leap.

MEASURING IMAGINATION

From what I understand, when doctors examined Einstein's brain, they found it quite ordinary. It wasn't much larger or more developed in any significant way than most people's brains. It was just a brain like yours or mine. Yet what it accomplished was quite extraordinary. Einstein once said, "If one studies too zealously, one easily loses his pants." I suspect the doctor who removed the brain came to understand the wisdom of that thought.

Einstein also said that "imagination is more important than knowledge." I wonder what he would have thought of current education reform efforts. Certainly we are putting a premium on knowledge, particularly discreet bits of knowledge—but what about imagination? We can't measure imagination. Einstein pointed out that "it would be possible to describe everything scientifically, but it would make no sense; it would be without meaning, as if you described a Beethoven symphony as a variation of wave pressure."

Not everything that can be measured matters. Certainly our emphasis on rigor would have puzzled him. He offered that "teaching should be such that what is offered is perceived as a valuable gift and not a hard duty."

It strikes me that much of Einstein's genius came from his ability to look at the universe and see it differently—with imagination. In the lexicon of brain research, you might say that he was a "lateral thinker." He made unusual connections and was able to take immense complexity and make sense of it. For example, his explanation of his theory of relativity is a classic: "When you sit with a nice girl for two hours, it seems like two minutes. When you sit on a hot stove for two minutes, it seems like two hours. That is relativity."

While Einstein is remembered for his scientific and mathematical genius, it was his insights into the human condition that always struck me. He once observed that "only two things are infinite—the universe and human stupidity—and I'm not sure about the former." He was referring to humans' penchant for war. Einstein was deeply opposed and spoke out against it with power. He once said, "He who joyfully marches to music in rank and file has already earned my contempt. He has been given a large brain by mistake; since for him the spinal cord would suffice. . . . It is my conviction that killing under the cloak of war is nothing but an act of murder."

Of course, it must be remembered that he fled Germany before the Nazis assumed power and later saw the work of his theories create the basis for the nuclear age. So he had convictions about war that were profoundly held. He offered that he didn't know with what "weapons World War III will be fought, but World War IV will be fought with sticks and stones."

BATTLES AND WARS

I suspect most of us have a higher tolerance for war than Einstein, but then again none of us are Einsteins, are we?

As I was thinking about him, I found myself thinking about the Vietnam War, a time when our nation's collective brain seemed to have been removed. The fact that my brain jumped from Einstein to Vietnam either makes me a lateral thinker or a random one.

Specifically I was reminded of the Tet offensive, which took place toward the end of the war. What some of us remember is that it was the turning point that convinced most Americans it was time to end the war and come home. What is so interesting is that, militarily, the Tet offensive waged by the Communist insurgents was a miserable failure for them. The Americans and their allies won that battle decisively—with a significant kill ratio in favor of our troops. Yet the fact the enemy could mount such an operation and was willing to do so and to take the losses they took disheartened us and led to our wanting the war to cease. It was a classic case of winning the battle and losing the war.

As we work on education reform, we must guard against the possibility of winning the battle and losing the war. We can raise test scores without increasing intelligence. As we gather data and examine our students' brains, we must not fail to consider the human cost involved and to understand that we are educating more than brains— we are also educating their hearts.

Einstein once said, "There are only two ways to live your life. One is as though nothing is a miracle. The other is as though everything is a miracle." Our children are first and foremost miracles and deserve so much more than merely having their brains measured and weighed. We also must see their hearts don't fail them, and that will take imagination from all of us.

This essay received a Silver Award in 2006 from the American Society of Business Publication Editors, Central-Southeast Region.

27

ADVANCING SYSTEM LEADERSHIP

One challenge we face in our business is that every time we figure out the game, they change the rules. Sometimes they even change the game itself.

Education serves our nation and as our nation is challenged, it is expected schools will address the challenges. That is why our curriculum is often more crowded than the highways at quitting time. It is also why our schools seem to weave and veer from one new program to another.

Over the past decade schools have seen a major shift in what they are being asked to deliver to our society. Since the beginning of public education in America, schools were asked to provide access to an education by our children. The idea behind that was as simple as getting a child to the dinner table. The feeling was that if we got enough children to the table, they would have the opportunity to be fed. In fact, most of the landmark decisions affecting education have been about access and opportunity. Our goal, in essence, was universal access—a place at the table for everyone.

AN OUTGROWN GOAL

As we neared the millennium, we met that goal. School was made available for every child, regardless of race, social class, learning ability, or citizenship status. Exclusion was no longer accepted. Everyone had a seat at the table.

The public education system is built around this goal and virtually every aspect of the current system supports it. Our focus has been on providing enough classrooms and teachers. Even our school calendar was designed to meet the needs of farm children who could be educated and still help on the farms during the growing season. We have been superintendents of schools—leaders of spaces and places. And we can proudly say we met the goal the nation laid out for us.

But a funny thing happened on our way to the victory party. The goal changed. Meeting the goal of universal access was no longer enough. Not everyone had the same opportunity to succeed. Everyone had a seat, but not all the meals being served had the same nutritional value. We had great gaps in performance for poor children.

Further, our society had changed so that a basic education was no longer enough to ensure economic success. The information economy calls for a much higher proficiency than was previously required. This shift to universal proficiency requires a different kind of education, a different kind of educational system and a different kind of system leader.

The challenge currently facing us is that the goal has changed, but the system has not. Our school systems are perfectly designed to yield the results they are getting. The current system was designed and engineered for access. It also was designed to sort workers out for the industrial economy—managers over here, workers over there. Those working in the system were trained to provide that result. The system is funded for that purpose.

SYSTEM OVERHAUL

Reform efforts such as the standards and accountability movement have not adequately addressed the underlying issue. Even when you change the expected results and the systems for tracking those results, you still have not changed the system itself.

As the economy shifted and businesses faced a similar need for restructuring they came to realize they could not get the desired results simply by setting higher production goals and different rewards systems. They had to fundamentally change the way they were doing their work. They changed their system—top to bottom, side to side.

If we are to succeed in moving education to a new paradigm of high performance by all children, we will need a similar massive overhaul of the system itself. The standards and accountability imperative is important but inadequate. You can't simply change one part of the system such as its assessment programs and expect the rest of it to change.

The "market-driven" reforms are even less useful. You can't create a more intense competitive environment and expect the system to change without addressing issues of capacity. All that will do is make the strong stronger and the weak more vulnerable. If we truly expect public education to yield a different result, we will need to change our most basic assumptions and practices. It has been said that insanity is doing the same thing over and over again expecting a different result. Public education must be remade to have that different result.

NEW TOOLBOX

That starts with leadership. We need to develop a new generation of leaders who come to the task with a different understanding of the job and with a different skill set than previously required. Being masters of space and place must yield to proficiency with connection, communication, and collaboration. Superintendents of schools must become superintendents of learning. We need to retool our current leaders to remake the system top to bottom.

When business made its transition, it didn't throw away all its current managers—it retrained them, as it simultaneously prepared the next generation with a different set of skills. Educational leadership needs that same dual effort—the creation of a new generation of leaders and the remaking of the current leaders into superintendents of education and learning.

School system leaders need to learn a new set of tools to change the system to a new way of working. For that reason, AASA has embarked on creating a Center for System Leadership that will focus on strengthening our current leaders and building the next generation. We will work in conjunction with universities and the private sector to create standards and training that provide the skills needed to build new systems of learning.

The center also will create programs and support systems for the current generation of leaders to help them guide school systems through the transition to highly performing systems for highly performing children. To get a different result will require us to behave in different ways. That starts at the top.

28

MAKING GREAT TIME
ON A LOST HIGHWAY

Yogi Berra once said, "We may be lost, but we're making great time!" At least I think he said that because he also once said, "I didn't really say everything I said." Of course, Yogi was lost because he is a male and everyone knows we never stop to ask for directions. As I considered the idea of making great time while being lost, I naturally started thinking about school reform in this country.

For nearly 20 years we have waded around in the swamp of school reform, fixing schools that aren't broken and leveraging change that is not necessary. Now, before all the true believers of the current reform movement accuse me of being a "status quo educrat" willing to leave children behind, I will freely admit much needs to be done to make our schools places where all children can succeed. Yet I think the standards-based, test-and-punish, accountability and competition-at-all-cost models of reform are at best wrongheaded and at worst destructive.

It's quite simple. Current educational reforms are based on a misguided, mechanistic view of the world. This view rests on the Descartian belief that the universe is like a clock where if you change a few parts, you can make it tell better time. A mechanistic approach assumes that by fixing pieces, you can fix the whole and that by leveraging elements, you can move the totality to a different place. (Descartes has been upgraded to assume you can punish people into performance.)

COMPLEX CONNECTIONS

My view of the universe and organizations is more organic in nature; I see these worlds as interconnected and this quality defies easy fixes. You can't fix organisms; you must heal them. Most school leaders readily understand the interrelated qualities of organizations. We notice that when we change 1 variable in our system, 10 others are affected almost immediately. We think we are changing our sex education curriculum, but we are really electing your next school board. We may think we are closing schools to reduce the budget, but we are really determining the length of our next contract. Everything is connected to everything else.

H. L. Mencken once said, "For every complex problem there is a simple solution and it is wrong." With this in mind, why do we think we can mount simple answers to complex problems or believe that all that's required is to change one thing (even if it is an improvement), and everything else will change? This thinking is the polar opposite of chaos theory. In this version, if you put one thing in order, the rest of the universe will snap to and get in line. I don't think so.

What the proponents of the mechanical view of reform have never understood is that those of us fighting it don't do so because we think there should be no standards or accountability or even competition under the right circumstances. It is because we believe these things are woefully inadequate to make the system better. You can't stop leaving children behind merely by testing them and then putting their schools up to ridicule for poor performance. You can't improve education by setting standards unless you are willing to provide the support necessary for meeting the standards. You have to make sure the children are healthy and nourished and exposed to good teachers while providing them with the right materials and curriculum.

We also understand that you can't beat people into excellence. You don't inspire people by yelling at them.

Mechanical fixes are easy—and ineffective. Organic solutions are hard, but ultimately they are the only way to improve schools. So while we are making good time on creating a system of mechanical fixes, we are lost in the space of an organic universe.

AWKWARD EXPLANATION

One of my worries as someone who must explain why superintendents do what they do is that I have to explain why so many school leaders have jumped on the mechanical bandwagon. Aside from the fact that we are all people who want to please, I think the answer lies in the metaphor of lenses. We all start with our lens aimed at the mid-range of viewing. When you are responsible for making things better, you naturally tend to zoom in to find and create solutions. That blinds you to the broader vision of things.

The only solution is to pull the lens back to look long range, to look at the world in wide screen. Only then will you see how what you are getting ready to fix can make one thing better and make a dozen others worse. It will allow you to see the connected nature of things and to resist the simple and wrong answers.

Einstein once said, "Imagination is more important than knowledge." We can't measure imagination. We must create interconnected systems of answers to recognize that everything that counts can't be counted. We must acknowledge there is more to education than data and scores and that simple answers to complex problems will help us make great time as we roar down the lost highway.

29

DIVERSE LEARNERS

O ne of the remarkable paradoxes of American education is how we like to talk about the value of each child, and yet we strongly hold to a system that yields a one-size-fits-all model of educating all those individuals. For me, this contradiction always has been personal.

In my talks I often mention three children that each of us is familiar with because we have them in our schools.

The first is that child who never seems to be on the same page as everyone else. He is always a few pages short of a complete book. No matter how hard we work he is always, as my father used to say, "a day late and a dollar short." The child just doesn't get it. We have titles for these children. Perhaps one of the kindest is "slow learner."

Then there is another child who frustrates us more than the first. We give the slow learners some slack because they just don't seem capable of mastering the material. The second child is totally capable—but she just won't do it. We know from her test scores that she is a capable learner, but her effort is not up to her capacity. We label these children "underachievers" and they drive us crazy because they don't work up to their potential.

The third child is a favorite. This child knows the answers before we give the lesson. She is bright-eyed and full of enthusiasm for almost everything. She can even stretch us. We call these children "gifted" and they make us feel successful as educators.

Personal Differences

Now here's the rub. I was all three of these children. I started off as a slow learner, not learning to read until third grade. (By the way, in the ongoing controversy over social promotion and retention, I get up every morning and thank God for social promotion because without it, I would be the oldest first grader in America!) Thank goodness, I was promoted until I reached Mrs. Spurlock's class so she could take me under her wing and teach me to read.

By the time I reached junior high I was such a good reader that I achieved "underachiever" status. I was seen as having potential but wasn't using it. I did well on tests and poorly in the classroom. High school found me hitting on every note and I became gifted. The school thought I was new to the community because I wasn't expected to do well.

What changed? The problem in retrospect is that I am a holistic learner rather than a sequential learner. I have to have all the pieces before I get it. I don't move neatly from block to block. I kind of wander the neighborhood until I learn the terrain.

Sadly for me and those who learn like me, schools weren't created for us. It has been estimated that only about 20 percent of our children actually learn according to the way we structure schools. Whether it is holistic versus sequential or kinesthetic versus auditory, many kids don't fit the molds we create for them. Given all that, it is just short of amazing we get the results we do.

I have driven more than one education reformer mad by suggesting that standards, accountability, and choice will not yield us great schools. In fact, they may take us backward. Rather, what we should be doing is creating schools kids want to attend. These would be places where learning is meaningful and engaging to the students. Learning must be connected to their world, their culture, and their learning styles. And it must be personalized. With the advances technology offers us, this is not an unrealistic expectation. Our goal must be to create schools that are exciting places and that really do value every child.

The formula for success is insight + incite = excite. We must work to understand and celebrate the differences our children bring to school. Not all children are gifted. But they all have gifts. And not every child we label a slow learner is slow. And if children are underachieving we must ask whose sin that is. We must develop insight into how kids learn and what motivates them. Then we must find ways of inciting them to action.

UNSTOPPABLE BELIEFS

I had the occasion a few years ago to attend a Tony Robbins seminar and, to this day, I am amazed at the fact that in a few hours he was able to persuade me and about 2,000 other people into walking across a bed of hot coals. I don't like to walk on hot sand at the beach and here I was walking across 12 feet of burning coals. He created such a strong sense of belief that we could do that feat that we couldn't wait to get to the coals. If we could instill a fraction of that belief in our children about what they are capable of doing, we would have created a system of education that would be unstoppable.

During the "fire walk" experience we found that as we approached the coals, we were urged to focus on what was across the coals, not on the coals themselves. In essence we became so focused on where we wanted to go, we had no time to think about the problems and dangers under our feet.

At a recent talk, Peter Senge observed that nothing in nature is exactly the same. No two things have been created that were just alike. American education will be "reformed" when we come to understand and truly prize the differences our children bring with them and be able to capitalize on those differences by constructing a learning environment that is open to different ways of learning and that focuses us on where we need to be as a system and as a nation. Then we will see that the whole truly is a multiplier of the sum of the parts.

30

BUTCHERS OR
TAILORS?

G reek mythology contains a story about an innkeeper named
Procrustes, who took in travelers. He had one problem: His
inn had only one bed.

When a traveler came to the inn, Procrustes measured him. If he
was too long for the bed, Procrustes chopped off his legs to the right
length. If he was too short, Procrustes tied the traveler to a rack and
stretched him to the right length. You didn't want to have to spend
the night at Procrustes' place.

When I thought about this story, I realized it pertained to how we
have gone about educating our children. We have offered them a
one-size-fits-all education, and if they didn't fit the bed we made for
them, the consequences were sometimes dire. As we consider ways
to improve our educational system, we must discover alternatives to
our Procrustean approach to educating.

NOSTALGIC YEARNINGS

Regular readers of my column will not be surprised to know I have
a poor regard for our current school reform efforts. I believe they are
built on a faulty set of assumptions about what is wrong with schools
today. When I talk to the media about this I remind them that when
you lean your ladder against the wrong wall you paint the wrong

house. When you build solutions based on the wrong assessment of the problem you solve the wrong things. Much of the current reform is about reaching back and shoring up what we used to do. It is built on the belief that we need kids today to be more like we used to be. Heaven forbid!

While I have my own forays into nostalgia, I also am painfully aware that when I was in school it wasn't a place for everyone. Many kids were systemically excluded and the skills I was taught in high school were what most kids today are learning in middle school. Certainly we still have our challenges. We have given everyone access, but children of poverty are not getting what other children receive as a matter of course. Unfortunately another truth is that much of what we give children today is pretty boring. The wonder isn't that some learn and some don't. The wonder is they don't rise in rebellion against the deadly dull experiences we dish out to them everyday that we call learning. This leads me to another criticism of our reform efforts.

Much of the current reform is based upon a belief that what is needed is "more" and "harder." We need more content, harder standards, more homework, harder tests, more classes, harder teachers, and so forth. This has led me to comment that much of what we are trying to do is bludgeon people, in this case children, to greatness. We are beating them toward excellence. Of course this will not work because it flies in the face of motivation and cognitive research. You can't scare people into becoming smarter or shame them into pursuing higher order thinking. Any system that is built on fear will ultimately fail because fear and coercion can only take you so far before they ultimately lead to breakdown and rebellion.

Further, the current system of reform lacks "beef" at its core. Yes, one needs standards. Certainly one needs assessment. But somewhere between setting the standards and testing them, we need to create a system that takes people toward achievement. This requires giving the kids who need the most help the most help— better teachers, good facilities, excellent curriculum and materials, and the time to take advantage of all that. Without this beef in the center, you have what Gaston Caperton, president of the College Board, calls a bread sandwich. Not much nourishment there.

PERSONALIZED LEARNING

Probably what we most need in school reform is an understanding that we don't need to reform it nearly as much as we need to transform it. We must rethink what schools are about and how we should deliver learning to children. The goal of transformed education is children who are eager to get to school every day—that the school is a place where they want to be.

That means schools must be engaging places where children are involved in their learning in active and meaningful ways. We perform best as adults when we are doing work that we love, work that has deep meaning for us. Why would it be any different for children?

That leads us to the need to personalize education for children. The best part of IDEA, as far as I am concerned, is the requirement for an individual education plan—a plan that was tailored to the special needs of the child. Well, aren't all our children special? Shouldn't all of them have a PEP—a personalized education plan, a plan that takes into consideration their learning interests and styles, and pace of learning? A plan that meets their needs as individuals? With the availability of new technology, it is not beyond our reach to think in these terms anymore. We know how kids learn and we can shape learning to fit their needs.

I love clothes. A few years ago during some of my travels, I was able to get a few suits tailored for me. What a difference from the off-the-rack clothes I had been buying. Tailored clothes not only fit you better, they accentuate your best features and compensate for those little bulges and bumps that most of us have. School reform has to be about getting our children the right fit and not about chopping them up to fit what we have to offer. We need more tailors and fewer butchers.

31

THE BIGOTRY OF EXPECTATIONS

As we grapple with implementing the No Child Left Behind Act, we should focus on its intent. While in my more cynical moments I wonder if the intent wasn't to prove, once and for all, that public schools are so flawed they are not worth supporting and that vouchers are the only alternative, my higher angels call me to assume the best of those who have promoted the bill. Certainly much about the bill merits support.

It is hard to argue with the idea that we should leave no child behind. We know that has not been true up to now. One great shortcoming of our nation is that we do leave a significant portion of our people behind and that has been true in schools as well.

While evidence is clear that we have improved school performance over time (significantly higher percentages complete school, increasing numbers attend college, etc.), we also must acknowledge that many of our children, especially those trapped in poverty, have been left out of the loop of success.

Those who support NCLB point out that past programs that merely play to the effects of poverty without setting higher standards have harmed the very children we wanted to help. It is also hard to argue with the notion that every classroom should be staffed by a qualified teacher. You can't argue with the need for assessment to ascertain results. It is even hard to argue that a school that fails some of its children while succeeding with the rest is not a failing school.

Unreal Expectations

So it is hard to argue with the law's highest intentions. However, I take great exception with its implementation. It was designed by folks who seem not to have been around schools much and who lack the practical understanding of how you make things happen where the rubber meets the road. Thus far the designers haven't shown much interest in working with folks who do have to carry it out. The law also relies on coercion rather than collaboration as its approach to dealing with people. It seems to equate achievement with test scores and accountability with punishment. And it sets timelines that are out of touch with reality.

But the biggest problem I have with the law is the attitude it assumes about people who work in schools. The president and the secretary of education both have talked about the "soft bigotry of low expectations." And they are absolutely right. Low expectations doom children to a life half-lived. Education is about helping them soar to their highest possibilities. It is not about clipping their wings. So it is right for them to rail against this form of bigotry. Anyone who works with children must see the nobility of their possibilities.

However, let us also be sensitive to the hard bigotry of high expectations for all while some are left at a disadvantage. I have put it this way before—it is one thing to expect people to pull themselves up by their own bootstraps, but first you need to make sure they are wearing boots.

NCLB presupposes a level playing field that does not exist in many school districts and for many of our children. How can you not leave some children behind when the schools and school districts they attend have been left behind for years? How can you have highly qualified teachers in every classroom when some districts struggle to have any teacher in the classroom?

Spouting Rhetoric

The sad fact about America is that we have tolerated and, in fact, created systems that allow and support tremendous inequity in terms of financing and support. Those systems were not created by educators; they were created by politicians. You can't have equity outcomes with inequitable resources that shortchange the children most in need. And educators cannot be expected to overcome the effects of systems they did not create. Simply creating a strict system of accountability that points down from on high and out to schools that are often "down and out" themselves will not solve the achievement gaps. Accountability is also appropriate for those who write the checks.

If one child attends a school where $3,000 is spent on his or her education and another child attends a school where $10,000 is spent, a different outcome will likely emerge. Simply excoriating the staff of that lower-spending school to work harder and to raise expectations is insulting and really rather silly.

The first year of NCLB saw a dramatic increase in funding. Yet less than a month after signing the bill into law, the president sent the next budget to Congress that was a flat-line budget for education. You can't create landmark legislation and then fail to commit to it in the long run. You can't achieve results simply by spouting the right rhetoric.

While politicians are worrying about making the tax cuts permanent, I hope they also will consider making that same long-term commitment to our children. Otherwise, the soft bigotry of low expectations will be hardened into national policy.

32

RUNNING SCHOOLS LIKE BUSINESS

B ecause I give speeches often, I am always looking for a good laugh line to loosen up the audience. Lately I have found one: "Why don't we make schools more like business?"

For years as a superintendent, I had to eat and sleep negative comparisons between schools and businesses. All I heard was that we should run schools like a business. If schools were ever to improve, we needed to watch and learn from business how they did things. We had the problems; they had the answers.

What a difference a few months can make. After months of hearing the "scandal de jour" from insider trading to shredded documents to doctored accounting and audits to phantom partnerships to lavish stock options and the like, I haven't heard anyone suggesting lately that schools need to pattern themselves after business. Gee, even Martha Stewart, that paragon of propriety, allegedly has been putting more than green lettuce in her salads. Now that Enron, WorldCom, and Adelphia have become fodder for late-night comics, few are suggesting we operate like these folks.

COMPLEX CONNECTIONS

Of course, schools and business have always had a complex relationship. We supply the future workforce and customer base. They help supply the money for us to run (although it could be argued not always their fair share what with the tax breaks and loopholes available to many).

Schools often have been used as the designated whipping boy for some business folk to cover their failures. You remember the *A Nation at Risk* report and the "rising tide of mediocrity" that was threatening to swamp the good ship of American capitalism in the 1980s. The failure of schools to adequately train our workforce to world-class standards put America at an international economic disadvantage. Of course, during the booming nineties no one came forth to credit the schools with the turnaround, so you will excuse a bit of righteous indignation on my part as I witness the fall from grace of those who had all the answers for us.

It is hard to listen to business leaders decry the quality of their workforce with one breath and then complain about higher taxes with the next breath as if there is no connection between the two things. And of course after hearing for years that "money doesn't matter" and that schools should do more with less and then seeing the obscene amounts of money that many of these same people have made boggles the mind and upsets the stomach. Further, as we struggle to teach children values, we must offset the example of incredible greed and dishonesty demonstrated by some of these same leaders.

DANGEROUS COMPARISONS

Now, lest I get too carried away, we must not do to business what many of them have done to us—to paint all with an ugly color for the failing of some. I am confident and hopeful that most businesses are not guilty of the financial shenanigans and blatant greed and corruption that we have witnessed lately.

We know that many school systems (and even associations like AASA) have developed rich and deep partnerships of mutual support with businesses. In the future, schools will likely be even more affiliated with private-sector partners. That can be a good thing. It is possible to do well and do good at the same time. We also must admit readily that we school leaders could improve many of our business practices and that learning from responsible business leaders could be helpful.

But we also have to remember that drawing comparisons is dangerous and that apples and oranges, while being fruit, are still not the same fruit and require different climates and care. Schools are fundamentally different creatures than business. We don't control our raw materials and we have to keep working with sometimes "defective" material. In fact, the glory of public education is that it is so often successful with material that would be quickly rejected in the private sector.

We also can learn some common lessons from the current struggles of business. It isn't all about money; it is also about values and human dignity. It shouldn't be about greed; it should be about goodness. And while many businesses got into trouble because they had a much too narrow view of accountability—looking good on the quarterly report—schools must guard against the impulse to score well on the accountability measures while we ignore the basic work of education—to help children grow into their full potential to become contributing and honest members of the good society.

33

NCLB:
DREAMS AND
NIGHTMARES

I t is my understanding that humans share many of the same nightmares, like going to a party with no clothes on or showing up for the final exam in a class you forgot to attend or, on the happier side, falling from a cliff and discovering that you can fly. Today, educators share a nightmare known as NCLB (or "Nickelbee" for the alphabetically impaired). Sadly, the No Child Left Behind Act is a nightmare in which everyone is naked while being pushed off a cliff because of poor test performance.

The Nickelbee nightmare has many variations. One involves trying to fill every classroom with a "highly qualified teacher." But in Nightmareland, highly qualified doesn't necessarily mean good. It means the teacher took the right number of subject-area courses in college and is teaching only those subjects. A certified chemistry teacher is not a highly qualified biology teacher. A middle school teacher certified as an elementary teacher is not highly qualified for middle school English. (Didn't we create middle schools so we could get away from the rigidity of the junior high school curriculum?)

The big exception is teachers who have taken no education courses but apply for alternative certification. The day they apply for certification, they become highly qualified. This is the magical approach to becoming highly qualified and proves that the bureau-crats who draft these laws have a sense of humor. Of course, highly qualified teachers don't have to be good teachers pedagogically, and they certainly don't need to be kind or compassionate toward children. They just need to show they mastered their subject areas.

The Nickelbee nightmare also involves explaining to your com-munity why your award-winning school is on the list of those that need to improve because you didn't make AYP (adequate yearly progress) in every sub-area with every sub-group. You might try to explain how progress isn't really progress because you aren't mea-suring the same children. You might explain that your school failed because one or two children were absent on test day, which dropped you below the 95 percent threshold for attendance. You might also have to explain why kids who have been identified for special edu-cation now have to meet the same standards as those who have not been so identified. In other words, students with special needs aren't really special when it comes to achieving common results. Makes one wonder why we have spent billions on special education when we could have just tested all those children to greatness. Oh, and don't forget that you have to make sure that students who come to you from Albania in third grade and who don't speak English will master that subject and the first three years of the curriculum in one year so that by fourth grade they are "proficient."

I could go on, but like swatting flies at a watermelon-eating con-test, it is just too easy to make fun of Nickelbee. The fact is that the goals of the law are fine. I haven't found one educator who doesn't agree with the high-minded goals of Nickelbee. I haven't met an edu-cator who thinks it is just fine to leave some kids behind. Many have swallowed hard in their efforts to embrace the law because it is an attempt to create more equitable expectations for our students. The president has talked about the soft bigotry of low expectations, and most educators I know agree that the phrase describes a real problem.

No one wants to see a single child left behind. In fact, it is a trib-ute to the nation's teachers and administrators that, despite the inanity of the law's details, they are working hard to implement it and make it work. From the coercive aspects of the law, one might think that the drafters thought children were being left behind on purpose. Why would people enter a profession as pressurized and thankless as teaching if they wanted to prevent some children from reaching their dreams? If policy makers really believe that, then we have a bigger failure to communicate than when we attempt to explain the law to parents. At some point, we need to discuss the hard bigotry of high expectations without adequate resources. It is no accident that most of the children left behind are clustered in poor schools in poor neighborhoods. That fact doesn't seem to get discussed much.

Further, no one argues that unqualified teachers belong in classrooms. No district advertises for poorly qualified teachers. The fact is that some schools are harder to staff than others. And we have to remember that private schools have made their reputations using uncertified teachers. (Come to think of it, private schools don't have the public accountability or testing requirements of Nicklebee.)

Educators welcome responsible accountability, and public schools have been open to public scrutiny on a regular basis. They are the one place where you can call public officials to account in a very public manner.

It is not the goals of Nickelbee that are problematic, nor its implementation and funding. They are fixable. We can modify the law to make certain that accountability occurs in ways that actually make sense by using the right assessment tools and measurements. We can raise the caliber of teachers in the classrooms by reshaping the qualities we seek in teachers and changing our incentives under a reasonable timetable. More money will help, but money alone is insufficient.

The fact is that the law has design flaws. The real reason that Nicklebee resembles a group nightmare is the lack of truth that permeates it. It is a search for weapons of mass mis-instruction that simply aren't there.

The fact is that we as a nation aren't really trying to leave no child behind. If we were, we would be doing much more than we are. We would recognize that we have an interrelated set of issues to confront and that they are bigger than a breadbox. Let me demonstrate by asking some questions.

If we really intended to leave no child behind, wouldn't we be worried about the kind of start children are getting? Wouldn't we see to it that those most likely to be left behind get reasonable pre- and postnatal health care so that by the time they get to school they haven't already fallen behind because of chronic health issues? Wouldn't we want to make sure that they are parented by people who can provide the kind of mental and emotional support a developing child needs? Might not that mean more parent education and the creation of a safety net around the parents of young children to help them in this vital work? Wouldn't we want to make sure that those most likely to fall behind get a better head start by having preschool programs available to them that develop their intellect by applying all we know about the development of young children?

If we really wanted to leave no child behind, wouldn't we see to it that those most likely to fall behind have the best teachers we can find? Wouldn't that mean "caring" as well as "qualified" teachers? Wouldn't we pursue policies that create incentives for our best teachers to work with those children who are most difficult to educate? Wouldn't we want to make sure that the schools these children attend have the best technology and learning materials we can find, and wouldn't we house them in the finest facilities? Wouldn't we make sure that different learning styles are accommodated to capitalize on their strengths? Wouldn't we make the school day and year flexible in order to accommodate different learning speeds?

If we really wanted to make sure no child was left behind, wouldn't we make certain that schools are so personal that all children have access to adults who know them well and who care about them? Doesn't that imply moving away from our fixation on economies of scale and efficiency and moving toward smaller and more intimate learning environments? Wouldn't we provide many different activities to motivate and engage students in learning so that they run into the schools in the morning with the same energy and exuberance as they run out with in the afternoon?

If we really believed that all children are going to be highly proficient by 2014, wouldn't we be seeing major shifts in funding to make certain that those with the greatest needs receive the greatest resources? Wouldn't we also be seeing a massive effort to build up our universities to accommodate the crush of students who will soon be able to handle university work?

Sadly, no answers are being offered to any of these questions. In our quest for accountability, shouldn't we also be holding the politicians and bureaucrats accountable for creating systems that move beyond rhetoric so that we could truly remake American education into a system in which every child succeeds and in which each child's hopes are allowed to soar? If not, we must ask, "Where will we see no child left behind?" In our dreams.

This essay first appeared in the February 2005 issue of the Phi Delta Kappan Magazine.

SECTION IV

LESSONS FROM THE ROAD

34

BAGPIPES AND A SPOT OF GRACE

On a recent trip to Scotland I was able to attend the Royal Military Tattoo. No, this is not a multicolored body engraving of a picture of Queen Elizabeth that says "Hail to the Queen."

The Royal Tattoo is an incredible evening, blending military maneuvers with a music and light show and is performed in front of the castle in Edinburgh. For most visitors the highlight comes when hundreds of bagpipers launch into "Amazing Grace." The haunting music is so eerily beautiful it could raise the hair on Mr. Clean. As you listen to that haunting music and think of the words, you are moved to the depths of your soul.

"Amazing Grace, how sweet the sound, that saved a wretch like me. I once was lost, but now I am found, was blind but now I see." The hymn is a song about sin and redemption, despair and hope. It has moved people since it was written by John Newton, who had been a slave trader but who saw the error of his ways. The song is a form of amends to those ways. It is an acknowledgement that while you can be lost, you also can find your way back, through grace.

Grace Sustained

The roots of the song are clearly spiritual and religious. It is about God's gift of grace to humanity that frees us from past sins. But there are other elements of grace we must consider. Grace is something that is elegant and that shows a generosity of spirit. Once, when President Kennedy was asked what quality he admired in others, he quoted Ernest Hemingway's assessment of bullfighters—grace under pressure. Leaders, who live under pressure, must find their own way to grace and then impart that grace to others.

The Tattoo is a kaleidoscope of color and sound and can't be fully described in words. You have to be there to fully get it. But it is a demonstration of grace itself. Performers and audience members come from all over the world. They set aside their differences and build off their own cultures to create a panoply of movement and sound that is like no other.

A fife and drum corps from Massachusetts dressed in Revolutionary War regalia performed, then a full marching band and a drill team of young Chinese women from Taipei executed amazing precision so that the outcome was closer to dance than military maneuvers. Next a military band from Russia dressed in drab green military uniforms, goose-stepping across the castle floor only to break into modern rock music accompanied by their own version of hip hop dancing. Meanwhile, images are being projected onto the wall of the castle, lights and colors are constantly changing, and fireworks are being set off into the night sky.

But first and last is the corps of Scottish military drum and bagpipe bands, which blends its ancient music into heart-rending moments for the audience. I admit bagpipe music is an acquired taste, but you haven't really heard it until you hear it bouncing off the walls of an ancient castle. Its plaintive sounds will break your heart.

THE FULL PICTURE

My trip to Scotland was a personal vacation—no visits to schools, no discussions with policy leaders, and no worries about the implications for American education. Yet throughout the trip I found lessons for us.

Scotland is a rugged land. Its mountains are stark and foreboding. Its towns are built of the grey stone that covers the land. Yet the mountains are clothed in shades of green and the deep purple of heather. Their rugged vastness creates a context for the lone crane or mountain deer that you sometimes spot along the way. It highlights what might otherwise be overlooked. And the towns are draped in a profusion of flower boxes and planted gardens set against the grey stone walls of the houses. The heather and the planted gardens are even more spectacular because they are set against the grayness of their surroundings. That plainness frames the picture.

We have to notice both figure and ground to get the full picture. Often in our work we are so intent on the details, we fail to see the bigger picture. Schools have been so busy complying with federal mandates they have forgotten to ask why those mandates exist and whether those in Washington are best equipped to direct the work. They have allowed themselves to be bullied into doing things that are not good for kids or teachers because they are fearful of not meeting the requirements. The result is we have replaced our flowers with shades of gray.

This takes me to another lesson from Scotland. On our trip, the tour visited the Battlefield of Culloden where the forces of Bonny Prince Charlie were defeated by the British. I found two lessons in those stark fields. The fellow that the prince sent out to survey the field came back with the wrong conclusions. He suggested it was a great place for a battle. It was—for the British. It was wide and flat and played into the British strengths. Up to that time the Scots had won every battle by using the mountainous terrain that they knew so well to their advantage. Flat isn't familiar to a Scotsman. This fellow was also the guy who ordered the wrong-sized cannon balls for the battle. They wouldn't fit the cannons the Scots had. It's hard to win a battle with the wrong cannons and no balls.

They entered that battlefield undefeated, but they were routed. Their battles seemed to be more about Bonny Prince Charlie's ambitions than about their own needs. They didn't really know what they were fighting for. They were undefeated yet demoralized and they were routed.

The battles we fight need to be those that we understand and are committed to. We need to understand the context, and we need to do so in a way that brings a spot of grace to those around us.

35

FINDING THE RIGHT WORDS

E ach year in December I reflect on the possible lessons of the season. A few months ago one Sunday evening I was watching an episode of *60 Minutes.* The show featured a segment by correspondent Bob Simon on a tribe living on boats off the coast of Southeast Asia. The segment referred to them as "Sea Gypsies"; they also are known as the Moken people.

Simon had traveled to their region after discovering that these people all had survived the great tsunami several years ago, despite living on the sea and on the beaches affected. How was such a thing possible?

It seems these gypsies are pretty much at one with the sea. They live on the ocean at least six months of the year and their children are born and grow up on boats. They learn to swim before they can walk. Children spend so much time in the water they have developed their vision so they can see under water about twice the distance of other humans, and they can stay under water almost twice as long as other people. Simon referred to these children as true "sea urchins."

Paying Attention

This connection to the sea allowed them to read the signs of the coming wave long before it hit. They saw the sea retreating, noticed the

131

sea birds flying away, and observed that the sea was not behaving normally. Furthermore, the Moken have a legend about the great waves that the sea god sends when he gets hungry. The waves eat the people to satisfy the god and cleanse the earth and make it new. There were elements in the story that gave them further insight into reading the impending waves and helped them survive.

They were able to get to higher ground or to maneuver their boats away from the impending disaster. Simon interviewed fishermen who had survived when the Burmese fishermen nearby them all died. He asked them how that was possible. They answered that the Burmese fishermen were so intent on catching the fish, they were not paying attention to the ocean.

That is the key to being present or mindful. When you are too busy doing, you forget to be, and you fail to pay attention to what is going on around you. The results can be deadly.

At this level, there are lessons for us. How do we survive the perils of the work we do? Can we find ways of becoming one with our environment so we can read its signs and act on its warnings? Leaders and schools are not separate from their organizations and their communities. They are part of them. But leaders have to pay attention and look at the bigger picture.

People are forever losing the forest by looking at the trees or being drowned in the ocean while they search for the fish. It is the big picture that must be taken. We cannot separate ourselves from the context of our work, for if we do, we sail at our own peril.

Time's Passage

Cultural traditions, whether in a primitive tribe of gypsies across the globe or close to home in our own communities, have a way of informing our understanding of the reality of today. Myths and legend become mythical because they are based on the truth of tradition. It is easy to dismiss them as "that's the way it used to be." In fact, the past is always just prologue to the present and we must pay attention or be engulfed by it.

The Moken's biggest lesson for Simon and for us was not how they lived through the tsunami, but in how they live every day. Simon was fascinated that every time he asked one of them their age, they didn't know. In talking with an anthropologist who had been studying their culture, he found they have no word for "when." In essence, they had no concept of time. They knew instinctively what our great modern scientist Albert Einstein had discovered, that time is relative—and not really that important. At least not important enough to find a word for.

This could go along with the fact they have no words for "hello" or "goodbye." They arrive and they leave. Their presence or the lack of it seems to be sufficient. No need to clutter it up with words that describe the obvious.

The Moken also have no word for "want." Think of how often we in America use the word "want." Imagine living our lives without the pressure of unrequited desire. Imagine what it would be like not to want anything. The Moken have words for "take" and "give," but to want something that cannot be taken or given is out of their understanding. They don't spend a lot of time fretting over what they don't have.

WORRYING LESS

Despite the world starting to impinge upon their idyllic existence, the Moken didn't seem too worried about it. They have no word for "worry" either. Of course, if you are not a slave to the clock, don't spend a lot of time looking to the past and the future, and don't really have a sense of wanting what you do not have, it would diminish the need for worry.

Words are the coin of a culture. Look at words that surround us—accountability, achievement, standards. They drive so much of how we spend our time and what we want out of it, and they sure make us worry.

Obviously, we live our lives on a different ocean and our boats rest on a less tranquil sea, but we can learn from these people we might call primitive. Maybe this coming year we should focus less on the ticking clock, want less of what we don't have, and worry less about what we cannot change. Not a bad way to launch our boat into the new year.

36

SNOW BLIND

Last year during the winter holidays I was driving across country to my home in Arizona. We left Kansas on a beautiful clear crisp winter day, headed for Albuquerque, New Mexico, to stay overnight before pushing on to Tucson. After 850 miles we were only about 60 miles from our destination so we stopped for a late dinner in Santa Rosa, New Mexico. When we came out, it was spitting snow. Not a good thing at that altitude.

We drove on for about 10 miles and were stopped by a traffic backup. Cars and trucks in front, beside, and behind. I thought there might be a wreck ahead, but I couldn't tell. We anticipated we might be stuck for a half hour or so and could still get to Albuquerque before bedtime. The half hour became an hour, then two, then three. Meanwhile, it was snowing harder. If we didn't move soon, the snow was going to be an issue. And by that time bodily functions were demanding attention. But how? And where? And why wouldn't someone come along and tell us what was happening ahead?

A WAITING GAME

It was getting colder by the minute and snowing harder by the second. Huge flakes tumbling all around and the car was getting cold. I had been smart enough in the first 15 minutes to turn off the engine to save gas. So, as the hours ran by, I restarted the engine for about 10 minutes every hour to warm up the car.

134

You couldn't really sleep—what if the traffic opened up while you were dozing and you missed the chance to go? We had figured out how to handle some of the body functions. (In the name of good taste I won't explain further—there really are some things you don't want to know.)

We waited. And waited. I was learning the Zen teaching of being in the moment. Where do you go when you can't go anywhere?

Then I realized that I was experiencing what our teachers must feel like in their No Child Left Behind world. They can't move forward, they can't back up, they aren't going anywhere, and the authorities won't even try to tell them what is happening or why. As they sit there in their classrooms, trying to survive (dealing with their own bodily functions), they are being buried in mindlessness.

It goes beyond frustrating—to a sense of hopelessness and mind-numbing emptiness. There is no sense of power over what is happening. And as they feel responsible for getting their children to safety and nothing is in their control, they may feel panicked and profoundly frustrated.

FLEETING HOPE

After six hours of sitting in the snow, the traffic started to move. It was now 3:30 a.m. We had missed our hotel reservation in Albuquerque but we were moving. Hope at last. We drove about a mile and everything stopped again. We had no idea why we had been allowed to start and now no idea why we were stopped. The routine continued.

Three hours later at 6:30 a.m. a highway patrolman came up the shoulder moving against the traffic. He was the first police officer we had seen. He was using his siren and winding his arm like a trail boss telling folks to move out. The traffic crept forward again and we found we were only about a quarter of a mile from a truck stop. It would have been nice to know that earlier. Or would it? Is it better to know something good is just ahead—or worse, knowing you probably still can't reach it, such as all students percent being proficient in math and literacy by 2014?

The police were sending everyone off the road into the truck stop. We joined hundreds of stranded passengers at one of the least pleasant establishments I have been in since my dorm room in college. Apparently, management had never heard that cleanliness is next to godliness or they were worshiping at some other church. And the overflow of travelers was overflowing everything else.

It was still snowing hard and was now about two feet deep. We were informed the police had closed the highway to Albuquerque. More waiting. Four hours in a truck stop in Somewhere, New Mexico (sounds like a country song). Then I noticed a few trucks were moving on the highway. Rumor around the stop was the police had reopened the highway west. Good enough for me.

We jumped in the car and started driving. Now, what was interesting was that with the exception of the few trucks I had seen, no one else was leaving the truck stop. They were waiting. Waiting for the snow to stop. Waiting for the highway folks to plow. Waiting for warmer weather. A couple of hours of slow and careful driving, following the ruts created by the trucks, found us in Albuquerque where the roads were passable. We then headed south toward sunny skies.

After getting to Tucson we followed the reports of the storm and learned that the stretch of road we had been on stayed closed for four more days! They were buried under four feet of snow. Four days of being stranded in the Truck Stop of the Lost. No food and no "facilities."

WHAT'S AHEAD?

So what did I learn? First, things are rarely as they seem—a sunny day can find a stormy night and stormy nights give way to sunny days. Things change. I also learned that if you are in charge of the traffic jam, let folks know what is happening.

Also, you have to know when to be patient. If traffic isn't moving, chill out. But then you have to know when to make your move when the opening arrives. Don't sit around waiting for things to get better. Sometimes they just get worse. And when you are going on a trip across open spaces, take food and water and an empty can for "recycling" them.

37

IS POSSIBLE?

In traveling to other countries I have been struck by how different Americans are from other nationalities. We stick out like a tall building in a swamp. We seem to be louder, more confident, often bigger, and sometimes less self-aware than others. While not everything we do is admirable, the way we handle the unknown is different and something I find laudatory.

When I was traveling in Russia, each time someone in our group wanted to do something that wasn't on the itinerary, our guide's response was the same: "Not possible." Whether it was to stay somewhere a little longer or leave a little sooner or deviate a block, it was always the same response: "Not possible."

Two incidents stand out in my memory. One came after a week of eating mystery meat and beets. We all felt we just couldn't face another meal spent turning over the meat to see whether we could identify it or noticing the overcooked beets and cabbage. We were getting desperate. We spotted a Pizza Hut downtown. We approached the guide about taking us there for dinner. Not possible. We asked the question, which seems to be uniquely American, "Why not?" "Driver is off duty."

"How about if we paid the driver extra for taking us there?" "Not possible." "Why not?" "Guide is off duty." "How about if we paid the guide extra for taking us there?" Long pause. "Maybe." "How much?" "Twenty dollars each." (At the time we didn't realize that was a month's pay for each of them.) Suddenly the impossible became possible. We left with our stomachs full of American-style pizza, and our guide and driver went home with their pockets full and a new appreciation for problem solving.

HIDDEN OPTIONS

Another day we wanted to go to the Moscow flea market. By this time our guide was learning the possible. Our bus was broken. It would run, but if it stopped, it wouldn't start. The bus carrying the second group was fine. But the party poopers on the other bus wanted to return to the hotel to rest. Most of our bus wanted to go to the Moscow flea market. What to do? No problem. We'll just switch busses and let the folks return to the hotel in the bus that would run, but not restart. No problem since it was already running. We would take the sound bus to the flea market. Our guide thought this was possible. She approached the other bus, but they wouldn't trade. Ugly Americans!

By this time we had Americanized the guide. She suggested that our bus could let us off at the Moscow subway, and we could take it to the market and back to the hotel. And we did. And by doing so we also got a tour of the Moscow subway, which is amazing. Hope that other bus group had a good nap!

On a more recent trip to Ireland our guide was going to offer us several options for dinner. But she laid out only one option and then asked how many of us wanted to do that. Of course, almost in unison, everyone shouted, "What are the other options?" Here we had another clash of cultures. Options aren't really options if you do not know all of them. Then you choose. In Ireland apparently, they take things sequentially one at a time, accepting or eliminating one thing before moving on.

The profound difference between how Americans process the world came home to me with two recent news stories. One incident concerned a young man who had figured out he could outsource his own job to India. He would pay the gentleman in India to do his work for a fraction of what the American was making, and the young American would pocket the difference. No strain and lots of gain. It worked so well he was considering taking a second job and doing the same thing to double his income. The point here isn't so much the ethics of what he was doing (which are questionable), but the creativity he showed in taking an issue that is driving many

Americans crazy—outsourcing—and making it work for him through some creative thinking.

The other story concerned a mother who was collecting cans of "crazy string" to send to her son and his fellow soldiers in Iraq. It seems the soldiers had figured out they could use the "crazy string" as a way to locate booby-trap tripwires in buildings they had to enter. By spraying the string in a room, previously undetected wires would catch the string and the soldiers could disarm the bomb—a very clever way of avoiding injury.

AMERICAN ENTERPRISE

The point of all this is that America is and has been a country where finding a creative solution is often the first response to a problem. There is always another way of doing something. Lay out the options, pick the best. If one thing doesn't work, try another.

As the minister of education in Singapore explained to *Newsweek* magazine, the reason many Americans outperform Singaporeans in the real world, even though the Singaporeans had better test scores, is that Americans are creative and innovative and they challenge authority.

As we endure these educational Dark Ages of high-stakes tests, a narrowed curriculum, and the search for a single right answer, let's not forget what we do better than others in the world. We turn crazy string into zones of safety and hunger pangs into win/win situations. That is pretty powerful stuff and worthy of being preserved. It is what has made us great as a nation and what will keep us great if we can get the misguided reformers to see there are other options to be considered and other ways of getting to the flea market. Staying dominant in the world is possible if we don't forget how we got there.

38

A PINT OF
GOOD SENSE

On a recent trip to Ireland I got to do what most visitors do—I consumed a pint or two of the Guinness. It is one of Ireland's best-known and best-loved creations. It is well worth the time it takes to watch it settle in the glass, which is quite a while. It also was worth my while to learn more about the Irish system of education.

Ireland is undergoing such a major economic boom that many describe Ireland as the "Celtic Tiger." There are plenty of jobs available and they pay well. Ireland has become a major player in the worldwide digital boom. Its closeness to the United States and the fact it is an English-speaking country has helped them as well. But as the country's minister of education pointed out to us, their economists have estimated that at least 20 percent of their economic success is due directly to the quality of their educational system.

There is much to be admired in the national policy that shapes their schools and drives their improvement. And as we discovered, the way they approach policy makes us envious because it was so rational. I longed for some of their good sense to be exported to the United States.

LOCAL AUTONOMY

While their schools are funded nationally, the federal government gives the local school councils great autonomy in how they run their schools. Just like our system, only backwards! Our feds give little money but demand lots of control. The Irish officials kept pointing out to us that the real teaching and learning took place locally, and the folks in Dublin couldn't possibly know more than the local folks who were actually doing the work.

That was just the first revelation—a system where those providing the pots of gold don't try to bend the rainbows by making the rules. Throughout the trip we were struck again and again by how the federal officials saw trust as critical to the process and collaboration as the best possible way of getting things done. What reasonable concepts!

The Irish value their teachers and try to pay them well so they won't be lost to the rest of the economy. And since they credit much of the economy to the work the teachers do, teachers enjoy a high degree of status.

Further, they are professionalizing teaching by collaborating with the teachers. They have developed teacher councils that are government sponsored but governed by representatives of the teacher unions and the government. The councils focus on the professional lives of teachers—how to certify them, how to develop them, and how to honor them.

This collaborative approach permeates all aspects of the Irish educational endeavor. In the spirit of full disclosure, they have few school administrators. Outside of the government "inspectors," there are virtually no administrators at the local level. The schools are run by the teachers and the local councils. However, the minister of education admitted that as Irish society is becoming more complex they are seeing the need for administrators, and she expects there soon will be a day when they are necessary.

QUALITY ASSURANCE

The good sense of the Irish was nowhere more evident than in how they handle accountability. Actually, they don't talk about it much. They have an elaborate system of what they call "quality assurance," which is the federal government's big hand in local schools.

But consider for a minute how different the notion of quality assurance is from accountability. In an accountability system, some people are held accountable by other people and blame and punishment are meted out. In a system focused on assuring quality, the work is approached much differently.

For example, the Irish don't just look at one aspect of student performance, test scores, they look at what items a good school should provide. The inspection process, which leads to quality assurance, looks at such things as parental involvement, learning support and professional development. They worry about the quality of management, the quality of planning and the quality of teaching and learning.

Of course, American critics of public schooling would call these things "inputs" and ignore them. But the reality is that they are at the center of the work. They are the "through puts" that make learning take place, and that is what the inspectors look for in assuring quality. They focus on what happens in the black box of learning.

OUT OF VIEW

There is one more big difference. The whole process is collaborative with the outcome determined by the inspector and the school working together. The whole process is to lead to improvement without coercion. The quality assurance process isn't to *grade* the school but to work *with* the school to find ways of getting better.

The foam on the top of the whole trip came when we asked the Irish minister of education how the nation handled student testing. She thought testing was important in the teaching and learning process but added, "Of course, we would never allow the scores to become public."

If test scores were made public, she said, the newspapers would start comparing schools because some schools had more children who had learning problems than others. It would be unfair to compare them because teachers in all the schools were working hard to do their best for students, she explained, and they shouldn't be humiliated in the public for things they could not control.

Say what? I think I need another pint.

39

THE ROAD TO HANA

On a recent trip to the lush and beautiful island of Maui, I had the occasion to do a lot of the "touristy" things one does on vacation. One highlight was to watch the whales that come there in winter to mate and give birth. One can see a mother escorting her toddler—all 15 feet and 30,000 pounds of him—around in the water.

One also can see competition pods of males thrashing around, banging heads and tails trying to impress the female whale so they might have the opportunity to get to know her better. Meanwhile, she hovers on the side waiting to see whether the winner is interesting enough to take home. If nothing else, this demonstrates that some things don't change much from specie to specie.

But one unique thing one can do on Maui is take the road to Hana. All the guidebooks insist the trip is something a visitor must do. So, of course, I did it. Now let me set the stage. The road to Hana is only about 50 miles in length. However, it has more than 600 curves and hundreds of one-lane bridges and other random one-lane spots where you can't see oncoming traffic. This is just to keep you on your toes.

The road hugs the side of a volcanic mountain and overlooks stretches of the Pacific Ocean. The resulting trip there is about a three-hour tour, about the same as the fabled cruise to Gilligan's Island—and I must confess there were moments when I thought the outcome would be about the same. Was it ever going to end?

A TORTUROUS TREK

Now why would anyone want to go on the road to Hana beyond being able to say you did it? Well, the scenery is some of the most spectacular in the world. There are dozens of amazing waterfalls and quiet pools. There are vistas of ocean and mountains that come right out of *Tales of the South Pacific*. There are black sand beaches, lava tubes and blow holes, botanical gardens, side hiking trails, and birds and other little critters to see all along the way. Of course the day we made the trip it poured rain so hard there were times we weren't sure whether we were seeing a waterfall or standing under it, so it was a different kind of experience.

Now, what is interesting to me was Hana itself. Once we got there we circled several times looking for the town. We saw a few houses, a restaurant, and a school. We thought we were on the outskirts, but once we drove through the cluster of houses back into countryside we realized that Hana didn't have any skirts to speak of. To put it kindly, there was not much Hana to Hana.

We had just spent three hours of torturous driving to get to a place we really had no interest in seeing. That's when it struck me. It wasn't about being in Hana, it was about getting to Hana. It was all about the journey. And that is when I knew there was a lesson there for all of us.

Educational leaders spend so much time focused on outcomes, results, goals, and objectives. We tend to ignore the journey. And when we get there, we often find there isn't much "there" there. We are so bent on getting to Hana, we miss the waterfalls along the way. I think most people tend to be so fixed on getting from point A to point B they don't notice anything in between.

A few years ago when I was diagnosed with glaucoma and came to understand it might jeopardize my ability to see, I realized I hadn't been seeing much all the years my eyesight was good. I made a vow to myself I would leave no sunset behind. I would no longer look out over an ocean or mountain vista or be confronted with a field of flowers and fail to see them. I vowed for as long as I could see, I would see. I would stop, look, and appreciate. Now, do I always do that? Of course not. Do I do it more than I did before? You betcha. Now I really do stop and smell the flowers.

DEFINING DESTINATIONS

As I observe my colleagues across the country dealing with the pressures of your jobs and trying to make the world a better place for children, my heart goes out to you as I watch you run past the flowers and sunsets. I want you to know that when you get to Hana, there really isn't that much there. In fact, it might not even be worth worrying about as a destination.

I have questioned repeatedly what we have established in this country as our educational goals. Are they the right goals and do they deserve the time and effort they are taking? Will our children be smarter just because their scores are higher? Are there other destinations like compassion and creativity that deserve attention?

Education must be more like the road to Hana—an experience of facing the unknown and the unexpected beauty of discovery along the way—not a forced march past all that which is worth seeing and doing.

The final great irony of my own trip to Hana was that after spending three hours weaving through the curves, looking at the waterfalls and pools, walking in the forests in the rain, and standing on the black sand beaches—after driving around trying to find more Hana in Hana, we still had the trip back from Hana to contend with. We still had the 600 curves and the narrow stretches to navigate. And even though it was the same road, the view was entirely different.

Our work is always going to be about the process—it always will be not about the "doing," but about the "being." We just have to allow ourselves to see what is around us and worry less about the final destination because there is no final destination—just lots of twists and turns and beautiful possibilities.

40

WATER AND ICE

As a child, I was late in learning to read but once I was given that gift I consumed books and dreamed of a world far beyond the little hollow of Davis Creek in West Virginia, where I lived. I wanted to see that world. And, to a large extent, I have.

Dreams led to effort and effort led to opportunities, and those opportunities have allowed me to travel to the ends of the earth. One of my recent trips took me there literally. I went to the bottom of the world, Antarctica, a place that lives in imagination but is largely inaccessible.

I wanted to go there because it would be my seventh continent, but I got more than I expected. As with most of my travels, I learned things I didn't expect to learn. Once again I learned a lot about what I do back home and a little about the place I visited. It is a shame that so many Americans have a limited experience with travel. Travel has made me more humble, less arrogant, and more open to the mysteries of the world and the people in it. I have come to understand there are lots of ways to be and each must be honored.

BREATHTAKING SIGHTS

In the case of Antarctica, I have to admit there weren't a lot of people there to learn from or honor and the lessons were more spiritual. When people learned I was planning to go, they usually had just one question: Why? I found my interest and curiosity were rarely matched by others. I heard a lot of, "Who in their right might mind would want to visit such a desolate and God-forsaken place?" "Isn't it freezing?" and "What's to see? There isn't anything there."

Oh, what you missed! Yes, it was a bit chilly but you can only visit there in the Antarctic "summer," which I must admit does broaden my definition of summer to the stretching point. It is cold, but no worse than much of the winters most of us experience here. And what is there to see? Nothing? Everything.

I have seen a lot of the world at this point and experienced many places of great beauty but I have never seen anyplace more breath-takingly beautiful than the mountains, glaciers, and icebergs of Antarctica. The mountains soar up above the ocean thousands of feet in shapes that may be seen on the moon but not many places on this earth. The glaciers are thousands of feet thick and so numerous they bear no names. Some are at water level and in the Antarctic summer they calve off into the water creating icebergs. Sadly, with the earth's surface getting warmer, that process has speeded up and more bergs are not a good thing.

Far from being God-forsaken, this is a place that is more like God made it than any other spot I have ever seen. It is the way the earth was before man came along and mucked it up. The icebergs, some as big as cities, were each carved into unique shapes and some were so deep blue, it requires a new word to describe. The water is so clear you could look to the bottom of the ocean, and the animals there live in a harmony we humans could learn from. And there is a serenity there that demands attention be paid to what is being seen. I found my usual frenetic Washington busyness being slowed to a near stop as I spent hours just being.

One evening we sailed through what the crew called "Iceberg Alley" and saw a parade of thousands of bergs, each spectacular and unique. They were God's ice carvings. One looked like Snoopy, another like the Sydney Opera House, and on and on. Here we were, a bunch of adults running from side to side of the ship like excited school children, but awed into silence with what we were seeing. The exception came when someone discovered a berg looked like something—much as we did as children looking at clouds in the sky. Often we would pass bergs with dozens of penguins on them—just "chilling" in the most literal sense.

WORTHY EFFORT

But one of the greatest lessons was not found there. It was gained by the trip there and back.

For the sake of honesty I have to admit that getting to Antarctica was a challenge. It wasn't so much the long flight to Buenos Aires and then another long flight to Ushuaia, which is the southernmost city in the world and sits at the end of Tierra del Fuego. The flights were child's play. It was the two-day cruise each way across the Drake Passage that was most memorable.

Quite simply, the Drake Passage is the roughest water in the world. Imagine a two-day cruise in a washing machine—set on high. To say you are tossed around is like saying that having a tooth pulled is a bit uncomfortable. One night I was literally tossed out of bed and awoke as I slid down the wall to the floor. Several folks were injured by slamming doors and by tumbling furniture. But once there, the trip was worth it.

That struck me as the real lesson—anything worth having or experiencing is worth the effort. And the harder the effort, the greater the worth.

Our work could be a lot like this trip. We experience the best of God's creations by serving children. Sometimes they are awesome to behold; sometimes they seem a little scary. But getting them to where they need to be is a tough trip sometimes but one that is worth the effort. And like the ice that is created from frozen water, the transformation of children from what they bring with them to unique works of art is the beauty of our work.

41

SEEING THE FOREST AND THE TREES

There is the old axiom that "you can't see the forest for the trees." While these days sometimes I have trouble seeing either one, that saying came home to me when I had the opportunity to spend time in the rain forest on two different occasions.

The first was several years ago when I spent a week on the Amazon where I observed the mysterious and dark forest flow past our boat. The Amazon basin has been called the "lungs of the earth" and concern has been raised as it is being obliterated by humans. Also, its biodiversity of plants and animals remains a source of many new medical discoveries. A lesson once again on how what happens in a distant place can affect us directly. If the earth's delicate balance of oxygen is upset, what do we breathe? If an obscure plant holds the secret for a cure for cancer, are we not all affected if the last one is destroyed?

As we went for hikes in the rain forest it was hard to see much. Our path was so overgrown with vegetation we had to hack our way through, and the mosquitoes were so thick they coated our clothing and turned it black. We were too busy dealing with the realities of foliage, mud, and insects to revel in our surroundings. On occasion we would spot an unusual bird or hear the cries of a monkey, but then it was back to the slog.

What we were able to see came with lots of hard work and sweat. Walking in the rain forest is not a stroll in the park—it is hard, dirty work.

BREAKNECK OBSERVATIONS

My second encounter with the rain forest was on a recent trip to Costa Rica. This time I got a different view. I went for a canopy trip, which according to the brochure offered a "leisurely trip across the top of the rain forest where one could appreciate the sights and sounds of the unique environment." Because I had already seen things from the bottom, the top sounded good to me.

They took us up a mountain on a Land Rover and after a short bumpy ride, we were let off for an equally short and bumpy trudge up the mountain where we were asked to climb a ladder, which took us to a platform on the side of a tree. This was to be the stepping off point for the "leisurely canopy tour." At that point one of the guides strapped us in a harness and informed us the harness would be attached to a rope that was connected to a very long, very high cable that connected to another tree far, far away. Our canopy ride would be on a zip line where we were to sail at breakneck speed hundreds of feet above the floor of the forest. Then we were to land on another platform high in another tree where the process would be repeated.

Before we stepped off into the void, folks were taking pictures. I am sure somewhere there is a picture of me with an expression on my face that clearly communicates, "You want me to do what?"

On the zip line you have to place your gloved hand above the line and press down to control your speed. If you press too hard you will slow your ride and stop many feet short of the platform where you will dangle high above the jungle floor wondering what to do next and why you had not opted for the leisurely day at the beach. If you don't press down hard enough you gain too much speed and sail full speed into the platform and the tree it is on—making for a sudden and unpleasant arrival.

The first few times you do this you are busy trying to master the technique to get the right speed and avoid embarrassing yourself that you get to the next platform not having seen anything but your hand and your feet. But after a few zips you start to relax and stop worrying about the mechanics of the ride. You realize you are not going to die, that it is really quite beautiful up there and the exhilaration of the ride is intoxicating.

GAP IN PERSPECTIVE

It struck me that the canopy experience was in many ways my experience as a new superintendent. At first I was so intent on just getting to the next stage I didn't have any sense of the journey. As I gained more experience and confidence, I was able to look around and enjoy the view. I think the lesson for us as leaders is to make certain that we master the techniques and mechanics of our work to the point they don't interfere with our ability to see around us. And you have to lead with a light hand—not too much pressure on the line and not too little. The right balance will get you where you need to go.

Another lesson from my rain forest experiences is that the view is very different between ground level and up at the top. The beauty at the top allowed me to forget the mud and the misery that was just a few hundred feet below me. Walking in the rain forest and riding above it are two very different experiences just like there is a huge gap in perspective between policy makers and those who have to do the work.

The final lesson comes from the understanding that just as the rain forests are the lungs of the earth and breathe life into us, public schools are the source of life for a democracy and must be preserved for our diversity and future. Finally, mosquitoes are an annoyance but they come with the territory. We have to focus on the big picture, not the bug picture.

42

ODE TO JOY

One spring I was asked to lead a weekend retreat on the topic of "Joy in the Workplace." It wasn't easy. First I am an educator and, as you know, lately it is sometimes hard to find joy in our work. Further, I live and work near Washington, D.C., where joy is the road kill on the superhighway to self-absorption. Finally, I had a lot of non-joyful personal issues on my plate at that point.

But I went to the retreat and listened and thought a lot. What I realized is that we tend to have a limited definition of joy. I call it the "Snoopy Dance" version of joy. You remember how the cartoon character Snoopy would express his happiness by bursting into a dance of unbridled ecstasy? I think that is how most of us tend to think joy operates and if we don't have that level of glee in our lives, we can't be experiencing joy.

The fact is that joy comes in many flavors and levels of intensity. Certainly the joy of a new love, the birth of a baby, or winning the lottery rank up there and deserve several Snoopy dances. But we should consider the joy found in a quiet moment of reflection amidst the din of confusion, the discovery of a spring flower, or a child's smile.

Additionally, there is joy when we have completed a difficult work task or we find ourselves in the flow of accomplishing something really hard. Joy is all around us. It is in the peak experiences of our life and it snuggles itself around the moments of serenity that are all too few. Joy grows in the connection to friends, family, or nature. It can be found in intense moments of passion or in the release from the dark moments of our soul. Joy is as much about Charlie Brown getting up once again after Lucy has pulled the football away as it is about Snoopy and his dance.

NEGLECTED FEELING

During the holidays we may confront joy as an expectation and we think about joy to the world. And yet, if you are like me, I always have treated it as a word and a concept, not a part of who I am or how I feel. We educators get so caught up in thinking, we forget to feel. We forget that at its core, joy is a feeling that can and must be experienced constantly.

A few weeks before my weekend retreat on joy, I had the chance to visit Brazil with a group of AASA folks. It was truly a wondrous experience. The country is breathtakingly beautiful and populated by wonderful people who have learned to live in the moment. In fact, it is such a lush and beautiful place the Brazilians have a phrase that "God is a Brazilian"—not because they want to claim God for themselves, but because they recognize how blessed they are to live in a place of such beauty and ease. The weather is almost always perfect, there are no natural disasters, and the food literally falls from the trees.

But all is not well there. Poverty and the distance between the haves and have-nots lies at the core of Brazilian life. The "favelas," or slums of their cities, are miserable places of poverty, prostitution, and drugs. Death is never far away. They lose literally thousands of children a month to gun and drug-related violence and the police are viewed as big a problem as the drug lords.

During the trip, we were passing one of the slums and our bus was struck by a bullet. Whether it was a stray or whether we had been targeted by the random violence that poverty breeds, we'll never know. All we knew is that the bus was hit and none of us was, and we felt joyful about that. We realized that joy can be dodging a bullet figuratively or literally. Joy stems from the short distance between death or an interesting story to tell back home—the two or three inches between a round hole in a metal frame or disaster, between horror and life.

SEIZING OPPORTUNITIES

As I reflected on the moment I realized how much we live our lives in that narrow geography between peril and possibility. So we are left with only one choice. We must choose how we live. And we must choose joy.

Near the end of the trip we visited Iguaçu Falls, which has to be one of the most spectacular sights anywhere in the world. Imagine Niagara Falls two miles wide set in the lush rain forest. We had butterflies landing on our heads and shoulders, and we were surrounded by rainbows. The power of the falls and the sheer beauty made onlookers throw their arms in the air and their heads back in joyful release.

The guides took us in a boat and after taking the requisite pictures, they had us put away the cameras and the captain said, "Now let's go get some fun." And we did as he drove us repeatedly in and out of the falls. We got about all the fun we could handle. It struck me that if we are to have fun, or joy, it is not about receiving it—it is about "getting it." We must choose life and we must make our joy.

As we celebrate this holiday season, we should be reminded that if our lives seem joyless and our work too hard, maybe it is because we haven't chosen to go get the possibilities that are all around us.

43

NEGOTIATING THE
PAST AND THE FUTURE

Once or twice a year AASA, along with University of Texas professor Nolan Estes, organizes an international seminar on schooling. We have superintendents, school board leaders, and higher education folks who spend a week or so visiting one or more countries, visiting schools and universities, and absorbing the culture of the country. I have shared many of these trips with you. One of the most recent was to Italy.

Some of my colleagues love to tease me about these trips—you know, "Too bad you had to go to Italy. Hope it wasn't too stressful." I point out that mine is a tough job but someone has to do it. Actually the trip allows AASA to be seen, not just as a national leader, but as an international leader. It also creates lots of discussion among the participants about what is going on in our own country and it allows me to think about the United States with new eyes that see the reflection from a distant mirror.

Now going to Italy cannot be considered hard duty. It is a beautiful country with warm people and great food. The hardest thing about going to Italy is making sure that your pants aren't too tight at the end of the trip. The second hardest thing is trying to find out what values underpin the country's education system.

ARTICULATING VALUES

The history and culture of Italy is so embedded in our own culture that going there makes one realize how much we owe them. English is heavily influenced by Latin, and much of our art and religion started there. Their schools also were a study in where we have been. It has been my experience that you can't really understand the schools of a country unless you understand the values of that country because the schools tend to reflect what the country most strongly values.

Wherever I travel I like to try to understand the values that are embedded in the schools. But this time I had trouble. Every time I asked an Italian educator what the values were, I got nowhere. Perhaps I wasn't making myself clear. Or perhaps it is just really hard for educators to know what the underlying values are. It led me to wonder, If I asked the same question here, what kind of answers might I hear? Can you state what values underpin American education?

However, while observing the schools I did come to understand that in many ways what we were seeing in the museums and historical sites was, in fact, the values that they wanted to preserve. It is clear that Italian children are expected to know and understand their history and culture and to appreciate languages other than their own. In essence, they are grounded in the past.

Where the schools in Italy seem weakest is in looking toward the future. Little technology is in place, and the schools' pedagogy is pretty much stuck in the nineteenth century. Teachers teach and students listen.

The week we were there the Parliament was debating and voting on its school reform legislation. I found two things amusing. The first was whenever we asked educators about the school reform bill they laughed. Not much different from Americans on that front. The second thing was that as they described their reforms, it was clear they were trying to make their schools more like American schools—at least like American schools used to be. A big emphasis was placed on moving away from a nationally dictated curriculum to more local control. They were trying to de-emphasize testing and while they were concerned with accountability, they were looking more broadly at what that means. And above all they wanted to inject more creativity into their students.

The cultural aspect of the trip took us to the ancient sites of Rome. Rome continues to be an object lesson for modern empires as it overreached and crumbled from within and finally succumbed to less advanced, more primitive societies. We visited Pompeii and saw a major city that disappeared in three days due to a volcanic eruption. Poignant castings were made from the actual preserved bodies of an expectant mother trying to protect her unborn child from the eruption of Vesuvius and a young child covering his face to avoid the ashes. Both obviously perished showing that despite our human instincts for survival sometimes we are just in the wrong place at the wrong time. Of course, we saw the magnificence of Michelangelo's work and wondered at how one person could bring such excellence and beauty to his fellow human beings.

MOVING FORWARD

Throughout the trip we stayed or ate in structures that were centuries older than this country. Even many of the schools we visited were located in old villas or palaces where vestiges of the art and culture of that earlier time mixed with today's Generation Y teenagers. This led me to another observation that the culture of "teenagerdom" is much stronger than the culture of mere countries. Teenagers are more alike around the world than they are different. That was brought home most poignantly while we visited a high school in Rome. It was the eve of the Iraqi war and we were serenaded by a young lady who sang "Imagine" with tears streaming down her face. The hope for peace knows no boundaries.

Late one evening we were returning to our hotel on our very large bus, which was trying to negotiate its way through the narrow streets of Florence. As it rounded a corner, it got stuck between cars that had parked too close to the corner leaving inadequate room for our bus to turn. We couldn't go forward and with traffic behind us we couldn't back up. As a school leader it made me feel right at home.

The driver, undaunted, got out and enlisted the aid of a couple of onlookers. Because cars are much smaller there they simply lifted the offending car and set it on the sidewalk. This led me to several insights. Sometimes you don't have to widen an ancient street and tear down the glorious past to make way for modernity. You just have to move the obstacles that are blocking you from moving ahead. And you can't do it alone.

So I am not so sure the Italian schools need to worry as much about creativity as they think. At least there is one bus driver there who has it figured out.

44

THE FANTASY AND FLOW OF VIETNAM

Let me tell you about my recent visit to Vietnam. It is exotic and beautiful. Most of its people are Buddhists, and they have gentle dispositions as sweet as the flowers that blossom over the countryside. Like most Buddhist countries, there is a peacefulness to it that makes you reflect on the tensions we feel here in our more developed country. But perhaps the greatest interest of Vietnam is the power it holds over American imaginations.

For Americans of my generation the Vietnam War was the pivotal event of our young adult lives. The names and visions we hold from the evening news are seared in our collective memories, and the passions and emotions linger just below the surface of our skin. Yet to go to Saigon (Ho Chi Minh City now is its official name) and to ride along the streets in search of that history is a largely fruitless quest. You just won't find many images from the war.

In fact, it was interesting to talk to the Vietnamese about it. We would ask about the war, they would pause wondering exactly which war we meant, and then their eyes would light up and they would say, "Oh, you mean the American War?" It would be our turn to pause for a second—not what we would have called it, but it makes sense, so we would plunge on in our conversation. Usually, the next statement out of their mouths was, "We were never sure why you were here." And many of us could relate to that.

From their perspective the war was about reunifying their country, which had been divided by the French. The issue here is not to revisit the wounds of that past time. But I kept hearing the words of a song from that era: "War . . . what is it good for? Absolutely nothing." We lost more than 50,000 young men in that war. The Vietnamese lost more than two million people and yet today, here we were dealing with it through the gauzy veil of history.

The Vietnamese continue to live their lives pretty much the same as they had before, and they wonder why we were there. Their dreams aren't that different from ours—peace and a better life for their children—and they would dearly love some of the modern conveniences we take for granted. Most wanted to visit the United States and they all wanted Americans to visit there. In essence the war means little today.

I don't consider myself a pacifist—I wish I had the moral clarity that those folks have. I think there are such things as just wars. But I also think we haven't seen many of them lately. Certainly, stopping Hitler comes to mind. I think that our efforts right after 9/11 to get the Al Qaeda fits that bill.

So the good news and bad news from Vietnam is that it doesn't seem the fruits of war linger; we saw no bitterness toward the United States or us, but the reasons for war also seemed strained now that it is over.

FASCINATING TRAFFIC

But the greatest lessons for me from Vietnam were about "flow." The greatest single image of the experience was watching the traffic flow through the streets of Saigon. It is a city of six million with four million motorcycles and few discernible traffic signals or rules. The traffic just keeps moving in this constant colorful swirl of patterns, lights, and sounds. And crossing the street always is an adventure. When and where do you cross? And what prayers should you utter?

It is like the old video game "Frogger" except in this case you want to miss all the logs. So you run and hop between the cycles and trucks with your heart in your throat and your life in your hands. But that isn't the way it should be done.

One night a friend and I were walking around. We had just had a conversation with a young Vietnamese boy who was trying to sell us souvenirs (capitalism thrives even there) and we were getting ready to make our mad dash through the traffic. As we stood on the curb, screwing up our courage, rocking back and forth in an effort to get going, he looked at us and said, "You don't know how to cross the street, do you?" We looked at each other sheepishly and said, "Well, not really." He said, "Just step out." We said, "Just step out?"

The boy said, "No, it's OK. Illegal to hit tourists here." I said, "Great, do all these people know that?" He said, "Follow me and just do what I do. Don't go too fast or too slow." And he stepped off the curb. I was reminded of the biblical admonition that "a little child shall lead them." So we stepped off right behind him. And it was magic.

MUTUAL TRUST

The traffic just flowed around us. It was like having a force field around our bodies that repelled motorcycles. I can't tell you how euphoric it was to just step out into that traffic and walk across those teeming streets and have the world flow around you.

You see the whole system is built upon reciprocity and trust. Everyone counts on everyone else knowing what they are doing ("not too slow, not too fast"), and each alters his or her movements to the other people. Pedestrians set the pace and the cyclists alter direction based on that. And everyone trusts one another to do the right thing. It occurred to me that perhaps the lesson here was that we would have fewer wars if we spent more time mastering trust and reciprocity.

But the real lesson I learned was about leadership. Sometimes you just have to step out. It may look dangerous and chaotic and patternless, but the only way you are getting to the other side is by stepping into the traffic and trusting the flow. I am willing to bet that if you can stay steady and deliberate and move with dispatch you will find a way to catch the flow and get your folks to the other side. If an eight-year-old could get me across the street in Saigon, moving your organization will be a walk in the street. And it will be a magic walk at that.

45

A WORTHY IMPORT
FROM SINGAPORE

The critics of American public schools love to compare us to other countries and then wonder why America can't do as well as say (pick one) Russia, Japan, Germany, or even little Singapore. They like to point out how much more money America spends on education and then decry our poor international standings. The latest, greatest comparisons have been with Singapore, which annually kicks our tail in international comparisons on math and science.

Now I must admit I haven't lost a lot of sleep over that. Singapore is, you see, a city state of several million people who are largely middle class. Their service economy workforce comes across the border from Malaysia in the morning and goes home at night. Singapore doesn't have to worry about leaving those poor children behind.

The country is democratic but very authoritarian in its culture. The fact that it is not as large as one of our major cities and is lacking our cultural diversity makes it a poor choice for making me feel guilty. Go find a country with our complexity and diversity that does better than we do and then I'll sit up and take notice.

However, that does not mean we can't learn from others—even those different from us. So I was excited to get to visit Singapore and see firsthand the educational miracle others had described. And what I saw was impressive.

DEPTH OF UNDERSTANDING

Undoubtedly their math and science instruction outshines ours. They put much more time and energy into it. In fact, there are other weaknesses in their system that might well stem from an overemphasis on those two areas. When you spend more time doing one thing, it means there is less time for something else.

Within the math and science area they do not try to cover the wide range of territory found in the American curriculum. They believe learning to do a few problems well and really understanding why you got the answers you did is much more important than doing a lot of problems without that understanding. I liked that emphasis on depth. They also spend a lot of time trying to think about the thinking they are doing—metacognition the psychologists call it. That was impressive.

But it was what I discovered about Singapore that our critics never share that impressed me most of all. First there was a recognition that the family is critical to having a good student and the schools depend on family support—psychic and monetary. Students are well-behaved and motivated because home and school work as a team.

Singapore itself is a very successful country. It is an economic power in a region of poverty. It is a center of enlightenment in a region of darkness. As one of our guides said, "We are a good boy in a neighborhood of bad boys."

Because it is rich and small, Singapore must guard against invasion by its neighbors who might envy its success. So it has a strong military. Yet the only thing in the Singaporean budget that had never been cut is not the military—it is education. Regardless of the strength or weakness of its economy, Singapore has increased its spending for schools every year of its history. Education is the No. 1 priority of the country in deed, not just in word.

DEEP RESPECT

The other thing that sets Singapore apart is its treatment of teachers. In Singapore if you want to be a teacher first you must get a regular college degree with a major in something. Can't you just feel the fluttering in the hearts of all those who believe that American teachers are bumbling numbskulls? Finally, someone gets it. Just get good people who know their subject and throw them in the classroom!

Not so fast there, Skippy. For after four years of college, if someone wants to teach, they spend a year at the National Institute of Education getting their pedagogical skills honed. For in Singapore they have figured out that you need both core knowledge and teaching knowledge to be effective.

But that is not the end of it. That fifth year is paid for by the government. You see, the government in Singapore has the weird idea that it must invest in developing good teachers. It doesn't mandate highly qualified teachers—it creates them. But wait, it gets better. These folks are paid as first-year teachers during their year of training. The government recognizes that people going to school have to eat, have a place to sleep, and maintain some self-respect so it begins treating them like teachers during that year.

But this is the best part: First-year teachers in Singapore get paid more than lawyers, engineers, or doctors. We asked about that and the answer was, "Why without teachers, you would not have lawyers or engineers or doctors. Everything starts with a teacher." Indeed it does. Now that is one lesson from Singapore worth stealing.

46

DIGGING MY WAY
TO CHINA

When we were children, many of us had the experience of digging in our backyards. I remember my mother saying if I dug far enough I would end up in China.

In those simpler years, we thought by moving some dirt we could travel to exotic places. Later we learned that would involve lots of cash, lost luggage, and airline delays. On a recent trip to China and Thailand those days were brought back when one of our guides said that when she was a child she and her friends would dig in the yard. Her parents told them if they dug far enough they would dig to the United States. It reminded me of how no matter where we grow up, childhood holds many common experiences.

I remembered my own childhood thoughts of how once we dug to China we would have to get used to walking around upside-down. Because our side of the world was right side up, the other side must be the opposite. China was also a land of scary enchantment. It was a place of dragons and great walls. It was a place of mysterious foreboding.

Isn't that how we often view other people and other cultures? They are different and less right than we are. And perhaps something to be feared. Once on a school visit to Australia I was shocked to find that the world map hanging in the classroom had Australia in the center of the map and the United States off in a far corner. How could that be? Everyone knows the United States is the center of the world. Of course we are the dominant economic and military power and our popular culture permeates all corners of the world, but we aren't all there is.

SELF-DISCIPLINE PERVADES

I came back from my trip convinced we needed to embrace China, but I also came back disturbed. On one of the school visits we made, we watched over a thousand young people doing their morning exercises to music—everyone moving in unison in exercises so perfect they seemed choreographed.

At first, our group was envious of the discipline and control shown by the exercise. But the more we watched, the more some of us worried. There was such regimentation and conformity that any sense of spontaneity was missing. They were together, but they didn't look happy. In fact, the schools and the society were fairly joyless places.

We were struck that we saw very few birds in China. And we saw very few smiles. It was as if the birds and the smiles had both taken wing to a happier place. There is an external discipline and control that permeates the culture that makes everything mechanistic and not very human.

When I asked different people there to tell me their dreams, they had a hard time answering. I finally got it. The dreams have gone with the birds and smiles. Dreams require freedom to soar. As we learned more about the country, we found that about 95 percent of the people consider themselves atheists. Even though China has a rich religious history, spirituality is mostly a relic of the past. And gone with it are their hopes for the future. Dreams also require hope to thrive.

A JOYOUS CONTRAST

We had an interesting contrast to that when we visited Thailand, a place where 95 percent of the population is Buddhist. It is also a country where smiles and joy are embedded deeply in the culture. I never have seen a friendlier, happier, or more centered people. And it became increasingly clear that happiness sprang from the rich ground of their spiritual beliefs.

When viewing a kindergarten class starting its day, we had a wonderful counterpoint to the regimented exercises we saw in Beijing. The Thai children were passing a candle from child to child. As the candle was handed off, each child's task was to meditate on the day, on his or her goals for their life, the kind of person he or she wanted to be, and how each needed to interact with classmates. It was a totally internal and organic process that created an inner discipline and a sense of joy.

The external process of China led to a disciplined world where people followed orders, but without the inner gyroscope of human dreams. The Thai journey is internal and seems to produce joy.

That led me to wonder about where America might be going in the days ahead as we work at improving our schools. Let us guard against the temptation to create a place where everyone dances to the same tune played by others while they lose the rhythm of their own dreams. And let us remember that spirituality is important in a good society and critical to a child's possibilities. That will allow us to unearth a society that will always be right side up.

INDEX

CORWIN PRESS

The Corwin Press logo—a raven striding across an open book—represents the union of courage and learning. Corwin Press is committed to improving education for all learners by publishing books and other professional development resources for those serving the field of PreK–12 education. By providing practical, hands-on materials, Corwin Press continues to carry out the promise of its motto: **"Helping Educators Do Their Work Better."**

**AMERICAN ASSOCIATION
OF SCHOOL ADMINISTRATORS**

The American Association of School Administrators, founded in 1865, is the professional organization for more than 13,000 educational leaders across the United States. AASA's mission is to support and develop effective school system leaders who are dedicated to the highest quality public education for all children. For more information, visit www.aasa.org.